PE   R'

TRENDS AND DEVELOPMENTS IN BUSINESS ADMINISTRATION PROGRAMS

TRENDS AND DEVELOPMENTS IN BUSINESS ADMINISTRATION PROGRAMS

Donald L. Joyal, D.B.A.

PRAEGER

PRAEGER SPECIAL STUDIES • PRAEGER SCIENTIFIC

Library of Congress Cataloging in Publication Data

Joyal, Donald L.
    Trends and developments in business administration programs.

    Bibliography: p.
    Includes index.
    1. Business education—United States.
2. Industrial management—Study and teaching—
United States.   I. Title.
HF1131-J78   658′.007′1173   81-15339
ISBN 0-03-060554-7   AACR2

Published in 1982 by Praeger Publishers
CBS Educational and Professional Publishing
a Division of CBS Inc.
521 Fifth Avenue, New York, New York 10175 U.S.A.

© 1982 by Praeger Publishers

23456789   145   987654321

Printed in the United States of America

PREFACE

Among the voices of discontent in the United States today,
none are more vocal than those facing the problem of finding and
keeping a job. Unique individual life-styles and constantly changing job requirements have made choosing a career more difficult
than in the past. It is no longer certain that a career for which
one is now training will still be in demand ten years from now.

The problem is especially acute with regard to manpower for
business administration. In particular, what sort of program best
prepares students for careers in business? What type of training
will enable the student to make choices and decisions of the kind
encountered on the job? Answering these and other questions requires that business educators must leave the isolation of the
classroom and establish personal contacts with personnel managers in the various organizations for which students are being
prepared.

That business colleges need to adapt their curriculum to the
needs of their students and the business world can scarcely be
challenged. The problem is how this may be accomplished. Accordingly, the purpose of the study was to establish guidelines for
improving the undergraduate business administration programs
offered by colleges. The study focused on formulating such guidelines on the basis of both an in-depth review of the relevant literature and a questionnaire study of the responses made by four
concerned groups: students in undergraduate business administration programs, faculty members teaching courses in such
programs, alumni of schools offering such programs, and the
business community.

Three main questions were paramount for the study.

1. To what extent do the four concerned groups identified
above and other interested sectors agree on the specific goals that
business administration programs ought to be pursuing?

2. How successful have various such programs been in achieving these goals ?

3. Is there an optimum model or program that can be recommended for business schools in general ?

Ten colleges in the states of Massachusetts and Rhode Island were involved. A total of 206 usable questionnaires was obtained from 450 individuals sampled. Each questionnaire asked the individual to respond on a five-point scale to various statements concerning business administration programs. Respondents were also asked to explain their reasons for certain of their answers and to recommend changes in business administration programs. Based on the results of the study, a number of guidelines were suggested:

1. More internship-cooperative business programs are needed, with more students participating in them.

2. Curricula and teaching methods should downplay theory and emphasize practice more, rely more on case studies, involve smaller classes, use instructors and lecturers with an excellent knowledge of the business world, and rely more on discussion and less on lecture.

3. Students should acquire more firsthand experience of the business world through field experience, work-study programs, and on-the-job experience, developing a greater sense of realism through awareness of the business world's emphasis on experience, communication, and mode of operation.

4. Faculty members should show more concern for student welfare and provide more effective counseling in career and course selection.

5. Students need to be much better prepared in the area of communication, including writing, speaking, and human relations.

6. More courses in the quantitative area are needed.

7. In addition to broadly based Bachelor of Arts and Bachelor of Science degrees in business administration, certificates of specialization in highly specific subject areas would be desirable. Such a change would give both students and employers greater assurance in the domain of job evaluation and placement.

8. More courses in modern management theory are needed. Such courses are intended to provide students with a conceptual framework adequate for interpreting the various social, psychological, and situational factors unique to the U.S. business administration scene.

9. More cross-cultural studies are needed. Studies such as those that focus on Japanese management, for example, are likely to give business administration students in the United States a deeper insight into their own situation by virtue of comparisons and contrasts with other cultures.

10. The present study should be replicated using larger and more diverse sample populations, especially those that include adult or evening school students who are participating in non-traditional and off-campus programs of business education.

ACKNOWLEDGMENTS

A number of individuals were especially helpful in the process of publishing this book. Their contributions ranged from informal suggestions to elaborate critiques. The author is especially appreciative of those who so graciously gave their moral support as well as the benefit of their technical competence throughout the research project's duration.

I am especially indebted to the work of Rafael Adames. His study of distributive education involved an excellent methodology which served as a model for the construction of the questionnaire employed in the present study.

My special thanks are offered to M. Singh, my doctoral adviser at Western Colorado University, and to his colleagues H. Earl Heusser and José Rabanal. Also, many thanks to Richard Juralewicz of Worcester State College. These colleagues and friends showed special interest in the manuscript and offered valuable suggestions during its preparation.

To my wife, Lorraine, and son, Wayne, as well as to both my father and mother, I offer my deepest feelings of appreciation for their encouragement, patience, understanding, and constant moral support.

To Joanne Keene, who worked so patiently typing the final manuscript, I thank you for your conscientiousness, patience, and assistance.

CONTENTS

LIST OF TABLES

TRENDS AND DEVELOPMENTS IN BUSINESS ADMINISTRATION PROGRAMS

1

INTRODUCTION

Life in the United States is currently being challenged by a number of issues revolving around its quality. The voices of discontent are numerous: alienated blue-collar workers, unemployed minorities, the young, the aged, the sick, and anyone else victimized by the frustrations of life in a mass technological society. Rhetorical, ideological, and partisan solutions to the problems of the discontent are formulated easily, "but truly effective responses are far more likely to be made if the obscure and complex sources of discontent are sorted out, and the lever of public policy is appropriately placed."[1]

One cause of the burgeoning discontent derives from the large number of potential life-styles characterizing U.S. society today. As their variety increases, the process of choosing a career becomes correspondingly more confusing. Individuals must weigh and balance different and often conflicting needs and desires. Accordingly, managers of organizations face "new and unexpected complexities in their traditional ways of mobilizing and directing human resources."[2]

Choosing a career has never been more difficult; there are simply too many choices and too many changes. A job that seems plausible to a student in junior high school may have vanished by the time that student graduates from college. Technological advances eliminate some jobs, while social trends change others. The security of entering the family business or profession is largely a thing of the past. An individual's family members are usually capable of offering little or no guidance in choosing a career. As a result, a new question has assumed major importance: "How can a student—or one of the growing army of midlife career switchers—choose a career that will be around 10 years from now and be enjoyable, too?"[3]

The problem is a particularly acute one when it comes to supplying manpower for middle management. According to Norman C. Harris and John F. Grede, training for management careers is an important function of colleges. To meet today's demands, most of the education for such careers has to be provided by colleges. "Well-planned, competency-based educational programs for paraprofessionals, semiprofessionals, and technicians are just as essential to good job performance in the middle manpower segment of the labor force as specialized and rigorous graduate training is to the future astrophysicist."[4]

The past 20 years have produced many suggestions for improvement and innovation in undergraduate business curricula. Grant funds are often available to those proposing instructional improvement programs. While the general objectives enunciated seem uncontroversial, how to go about achieving those objectives is not.[5] According to Frank K. Flaumenhaft, who investigated undergraduate business school curricula, "what is of concern to us is the almost total absence of recent articles . . . little is known about where college business education is, and less is known about where it is headed."[6]

These considerations suggest a crucial question: What sort of program best prepares students for careers in business? A related question concerns the core of studies including a student's concentrated major. Does it prepare the student adequately to approach his job and the decisions and choices that he is going to confront on the job? Don L. James and Ronald L. Decker[7] present evidence that industry personnel officers regard the core-plus-concentration approach as less desirable than one including fewer courses in a major but a larger number of courses in all functional areas.

One idea meeting with increasing favor is the principle that vocational educators must leave the isolation of the classroom and establish face-to-face liaison with personnel managers and shop supervisors in their particular curriculum industries.[8] The idea is a singularly natural one at a time when business is diversifying its support of higher education to include counseling of students, faculty members, and administrators, as well as cooperative efforts.[9]

In light of the background just sketched and in view of the general pressure to which business colleges are being subjected to adapt their curricula to the needs of the individuals they are serving if the colleges are to survive,[10] it becomes clear that more data are urgently needed concerning the issues underlying the scope and nature of undergraduate business administration programs. Of special concern for the present study was the manner in which a school's students, alumni, faculty members, and the surrounding business community view certain fundamental issues. A lack of consensus among these four groups may partly account for existing problems. Accordingly, it was necessary to find out what the views of these special groups were, subjecting them to a comparative analysis.

STATEMENT OF THE PROBLEM

Stated succinctly, the problem of the study was that of establishing guidelines for making meaningful decisions concerning curricula and special emphases in collegiate business administration programs. The study sought to formulate these guidelines through the medium of an in-depth review of the literature relevant to the specified problem and on the basis of an empirical study of responses from four concerned groups: students in undergraduate business administration programs, faculty members teaching courses in such programs, alumni of schools offering such programs, and the business community.

PROBLEM QUESTIONS

The study was designed to answer three major particularized questions.

1. To what extent do the four concerned groups identified above and other interested sectors agree on the specific goals that business administration programs ought to be pursuing?

2. How successful have various such programs been in achieving these goals?

3. Is there an optimum model or program which can be recommended for business schools in general?

STATEMENT OF THE PURPOSE

The purpose of the study was to provide ways and means for improving business administration programs through a comprehensive review of the relevant literature and through an empirical field study. More specifically, its purpose was to construct an optimum model or program that could be recommended to business schools in general. The author hoped that such a model would be especially useful to the professionals responsible for setting up collegiate business administration programs. A subsidiary but related purpose of the proposed study was to evaluate various existing programs and their comparative degrees of success or failure in meeting the current needs of the business community.

The author selected the proposed subject because of the importance attached to satisfying current business community needs and his perception of the possible serious inadequacy of existing business administration programs. The author believed that the research design used was the one most likely to produce the desired problem solution.

In the process of answering the first question, the empirical part of the study asked the four study groups to express their opinions concerning the following nine aspects of business administration programs:

1. What purpose should a business administration program pursue?
2. Who should determine the nature and scope of a collegiate business administration program: the faculty, the students, or the business community?
3. What criteria should govern admission of students into business administration programs?
4. What should the role of the business administration faculty be? Should it provide vocational career counseling, advise students in course selection, and/or work closely with the business community?
5. How effective are business administration programs in preparing students for actual jobs and in increasing their likelihood of obtaining jobs?

6. How relevant to job requirements are most current business administration programs?

7. How important is a business internship–cooperative program as part of the business administration curriculum?

8. How do the sample members evaluate the business administration programs with which they are familiar?

9. What changes would the various sample groups like to see made in existing business administration programs?

The second question was answered on the basis of the empirical part of the study, the author's own experience, and the literature review. By analyzing the answers to the first two questions, the author constructed a preferred model for collegiate business administration programs, thereby answering the final question.

PERFORMANCE OBJECTIVES

The author of this study attempted to achieve the following performance objectives:

1. To describe the findings reported in the relevant literature in a fashion reflecting that literature accurately;

2. To evaluate the adequacy with which the conclusions reached were supported by the data presented in the literature reviewed in Chapter 2 in a manner consistent with current research methods in education and the social sciences;

3. To assess the adequacy of various existing business administration programs and their comparative degrees of success or failure in meeting the current needs of the business community in order to help establish a rationale for the study;

4. To apply standard statistical techniques such as chi-square analyses and t-tests to interpreting the empirical data gathered in the study;

5. To analyze the views of the four subject groups of the empirical part of the study to find out what the differences are between the perceptions and interests of these groups;

6. To interpret and synthesize the answers to open-ended questions included in the study questionnaires in such a manner as to represent faithfully the attitudes of the questionnaire respondents;

7. To summarize the empirical part of the study in an orderly, logical fashion, permitting others to replicate it on the basis of the author's summary;

8. To compare data with a nationwide base reported in the relevant literature in order to arrive at conclusions applicable throughout the United States;

9. To establish useful guidelines for making meaningful decisions concerning curricula and special emphases in collegiate business administration programs as a preliminary to constructing a preferred (optimum) model of business administration programs;

10. To develop a preferred (optimum) model of business administration programs on the basis of both the literature reviewed and the empirical data gathered by the study, one that can be recommended to business schools generally.

DEFINITIONS OF TERMS

A number of terms had special importance for the study.

Admission criteria: The criteria used in admitting a student into a collegiate business administration program.

Business administration program: Any academic or college course of study presumably preparing a student for the area of business administration.

Business environment: The world of business with its unique mode of functioning. Students are often inadequately prepared for that environment because they are unfamiliar with the pragmatics of managing in a specific business environment, including its office politics and problems of communication.

Business involvement: A close relationship between both curriculum and faculty and the actual business world. Faculty business involvement is essential for improving the quality of business courses, reducing purely theoretical orientations, and introducing a greater pragmatic involvement.

Career counseling: Counseling of business students about the nature of a career in business. Such counseling involves helping the student choose his special field of interest and decide what its possibilities are for him.

Communication skill: Ability to deal with others effectively. Such skill includes reading and writing skills, as well as social skills.

Community input: The information or opinions obtained from the business community regarding program determinants and admission criteria for business administration programs.

Computer technology: The knowledge needed by business students to understand and operate various automated systems based on electronic computers. This technology requires offering highly specialized courses covering topics ranging from data-processing systems to writing computer programs.

Concentrated major: Some delimited, narrow field of specialization in which the student spends much or most of his time and effort.

Core program: A set of courses required of all students in a particular area of study or in a given business administration program.

Faculty input: The information or opinions obtained from the faculty members of a college regarding program determinants and admission criteria for business administration programs.

Internship-cooperative experience: Actual business experience acquired by a business school student in cooperation with some business firm.

Program determinants: The specific group of individuals determining what should be taught in a business administration program; in the case of the proposed study, students, faculty members, alumni, and/or the business community.

Program relevance: The degree of a collegiate business administration program's usefulness to students and the business community or of its congruence with their needs.

Student input: The information or opinions obtained from college students regarding program determinants and admission criteria for business administration programs.

Theoretical orientation: A business course orientation toward the theoretical as opposed to the practical aspects of business.

LIMITATIONS AND DELIMITATIONS

The study sample was limited to ten colleges in New England. While fixed-scale responses on the questionnaires delimited the data to a certain degree, a fuller range of data was provided for in the form of open-ended questions included in each of the four questionnaires. The sample response was large enough so as not to limit unduly the validity of the conclusions reached about it. Although the conclusions reached were necessarily limited to the study sample, it was the author's judgment that they were equally applicable to other regions of the United States. This potential limitation was largely offset by basing the preferred model partially on an in-depth review of the available relevant literature.

NOTES

1. Work in America, Report for the Department of Health, Education and Welfare (Cambridge, Mass.: MIT Press, 1976), p. xv.

2. John Van Maanen, Edgar H. Schrein, and Lottie Bailyn, "The Shape of Things to Come: A New Look at Organizational Careers," in Managing Career Development, ed. Marilyn A. Morgan (New York: D. Van Nostrand, 1980), p. 3.

3. Maureen Croteau, "Deadends Waylay the Unwary Seeker," The Providence Sunday Journal (Rhode Island), November 24, 1979, p. E3.

4. Norman C. Harris and John F. Grede, Career Education in Colleges (San Francisco: Jossey-Bass, 1977), p. 13.

5. Joseph W. McGuire, "The Collegiate Business School Today: Whatever Happened to the World We Knew?" Collegiate News and Views 25 (Spring 1972): 1-5.

6. Frank K. Flaumenhaft, "The Undergraduate Curriculum in Business Education," Collegiate News and Views 31 (Fall 1977): 17.

7. Don L. James and Ronald L. Decker, "Does Business Student Preparation Satisfy Personnel Officers?" Collegiate News and Views 27 (Spring 1974): 26-29.

8. Clifford L. Rall and Frank E. O'Brien, Methods and Procedures for Job Identification and Placement Based upon Industrial Needs (Washington, D.C.: Office of Education, August 21, 1977).

9. James E. Conner, "Business Broadens Its Support," College and University Journal 10 (May 1971): 8-9.

10. Ridley J. Gros, "The Communications Package in the Business Curriculum: Why?" ABCA Bulletin 39 (December 1976): 5-8.

2

REVIEW OF LITERATURE

A typical business administration program requires concentration on accounting, finance, marketing, economics, personnel, general management, or systems management. Some colleges award a general Bachelor of Science (B.S.) degree in business administration with a concentration in one of the aforementioned areas, while other colleges award a concentrated B.S. degree entirely within one area. Some colleges require a core program for all B.S. degrees in business administration. For instance, Bryant College in Smithfield, Rhode Island,[1] lists the following courses as comprising an undergraduate core program:

Courses	Semester Hours
Fundamental Accounting I and II	6
English Composition I and II	6
Microeconomic Principles	3
Macroeconomic Principles	3
College Algebra for Business and Calculus for Business	6
Introduction to Computer Data Processing	3
Principles of Management	3
Principles of Marketing	3
Total	33

Until the very early 1970s, few Massachusetts or Rhode Island colleges offered degrees in business administration or in management. More recently, these colleges have participated in a significant shift away from liberal arts programs and toward business administration programs.[2] At the same time, the conviction has spread that many business administration programs are not meeting the perceived needs of students and of the business community. The author's personal perceptions and feedback from others suggest that business school graduates are not sufficiently specialized in the principal areas of business administration. Students, faculty members, and alumni all realize that many students are not being prepared well for the work they will do after graduation. The Ford and Carnegie reports provide a particularly good overview and background of the problem.

THE FORD AND CARNEGIE REPORTS

In 1959 two excellent studies of collegiate business programs were conducted. The Ford Foundation funded a study by Robert A. Gordon and James E. Howell,[3] while the Carnegie Corporation of New York supported a study by Frank Pierson et al.[4] These two independent investigations were very similar in scope, content, and conclusions. They both found a need for upgrading the overall quality of business students and for broadening the undergraduate business curriculum in order to achieve a balance between vocational or professional courses and the general education represented by the typical liberal arts program.

The two reports had a direct influence on the subsequent curricula of college business programs. John J. Clark and Blaise J. Opulente reported that their net effect was to liberalize curricula at the expense of specialization.[5] At the same time, the reports emphasized the need for upgrading the quality of business students. Flaumenhaft believes that this goal has been pursued by established schools. "Competition for students that has accompanied the rapid growth of higher education in general, and schools and departments of business in particular, has greatly hampered the efforts of the new arrivals to conform to the high standards advocated in the Ford Foundation reports and their supporters."[6]

Frank Watson made a follow-up study of the Ford and Carnegie reports limiting his focus to the curriculum of undergraduate business education.[7] Basing his recommendations on the needs of

businessmen rather than on prevailing educational theory, he concluded that three qualities are essential for success in business:
the ability to communicate, human relations skills, and the ability
to solve problems.

Skill in these areas is something of an art. Flaumenhaft
believes that developing these skills is most likely if the business
curriculum includes courses in English, business communication,
the behavioral sciences, problem solving, and the case method of
decision making.[8] Herman Berliner[9] conducted studies supporting both Watson and Flaumenhaft on that score. Roger Gregoire
likewise concluded that the acquisition of skills in communication,
problem solving, and human relations was of the utmost importance for business students.[10] Specifically, he recommended that
the business curriculum include courses in native-language rhetoric; the sciences (learning the scientific methodology); the social
sciences, including economics, sociology, and psychology; foreign
languages; and practical studies such as accounting, statistical
analysis and programming, and business finance. Some authorities recommend much more training in quantitative methods including the differential and integral calculus of one variable.

By 1972 it was evident that many, if not most, schools of
business had tried implementing the recommendations of the
Carnegie and Ford studies by placing greater emphasis on nonvo-
cational subjects. Andrew C. Wallace, among many others holding similar opinions, conducted studies of large corporation
presidents and others with respect to the attributes most desired
in college recruits.[11] Wallace's poll convinced him that executive
preference was for more real world training with decidedly less
emphasis on theoretical research.

Another response to trends generated by the two 1959 foundation reports was voiced by D. Berry who wanted business curricula
to cater to the real needs of business. "Management education in
elite American schools is dying . . . because it is being sucked
into academic respectability."[12]

Flaumenhaft finds that even though liberal arts and science
courses remain firmly entrenched in most business programs,
many new business courses are finding their way into the curriculum. Included are courses in communications, public and private
institutional management, criminal justice, operations research,
computer science, finance, data processing, specialized retailing
programs, small business management, and international business. Flaumenhaft contends that the new courses reflect the desire of business students to acquire marketable skills. However,

"what is of concern to us is the almost total absence of recent articles and/or research dealing with the current curriculum in collegiate business programs."[13]

Attempts to devise new programs have, however, been made. One especially significant recent effort is that of the University of Wisconsin-Eau Claire program.

THE UNIVERSITY OF WISCONSIN-
EAU CLAIRE PROGRAM

In discussing a new program in business administration developed at the University of Wisconsin-Eau Claire, William E. Cayley and Thomas W. Harold[14] pinpoint a number of problems. The authors find that surveys of typical such programs show a central core of business/economic courses required of all majors in the school of business. Beyond the core, individual majors require a concentration of courses exclusively in their respective functional areas.

Cayley and Harold ask whether this kind of programming represents the best possible way of preparing students for careers in business. The authors cite data by T. R. Brannen[15] indicating that a high degree of specialization may be undesirable because large numbers of students in a given major accept entry-level positions in other functional areas (for example, a management major may work in a financial or marketing area), and after five years a majority of graduates will have changed jobs (many of them more than once), moving into areas different from their academic majors.

Cayley and Harold believe that the core with the concentrated major does not prepare a student adequately to approach a job and the various decisions and choices that one will encounter on the job. They argue that, in most cases, a student's first course in a given area (often the only course in nonmajor areas under the concentrated approach) serves only one or two purposes. First, it is probably a survey course designed to cover a broad functional area superficially. Second, it is also probably only a vocabulary builder and concept familiarizer within that business area. Whatever the case, the student does not acquire a thorough grasp of the business function involved or of its relationship to other functional areas.

In essence, we are saying that a well prepared graduate of an undergraduate business administration

> program should be familiar with more than the con-
> cepts, vocabulary, and tools of business. He/she
> should also have a greater awareness of interde-
> pendency among the functional areas than is afforded
> by the typical approach.[16]

The authors cite James and Decker's belief that most industries regard the core-plus-concentration approach as less desirable than one with fewer courses in a major and greater coverage
in all the functional areas.[17] James and Decker's favored curriculum consists of 60 semester credits: three hours each in statistics
and business communication; six hours each in accounting, finance,
marketing, management, data processing, economics, and business law; and a total of twelve hours in office administration,
transportation, ethics, insurance, real estate, and internship.

Cayley and Harold believe that such a program would yield
"product homogeneity" but question the value of a high degree of
specialization in any of the functional areas. By contrast, they describe a new 60-hour course that they contend provides the student
with a better background for pursuing a career in business. In
their program, the students enter second (and in some instances,
third) courses in all functional areas beyond the school of business
core; as well, they have the opportunity to specialize in one of the
functional areas. Specifically, they point out that the typical
business administration program requires 36 hours in a basic
business core program and 24 hours in requirements/electives in
the major area. The Cayley and Harold program requires 39 hours
in the basic business core, just nine hours in requirements and
electives in a major area, and three hours each in quantitative
analysis for business decisions, managerial accounting, a second
marketing course, a second finance course, and a second management course, all added to the core.

Students in the new program are still required to take the
basic core of courses (accounting, economics, data processing,
statistics, business law, and the introductory management, marketing, and finance courses, and a quantitative analysis course).
The uniqueness of the new program is that every student in business
administration must take a third accounting course and a second
course in finance, management, and marketing. Students still have
the opportunity to study their area of major interest while gaining
additional understanding and appreciation of related functional
areas.

The authors admit to some concern about undertaking the new program. Two fundamental questions were asked: Would they be overstructuring, thereby disallowing the student sufficient flexibility? Would such overstructuring have an unduly restrictive impact on students wanting to minor, for example, in accounting? With the options available in the new program, the authors believe that flexibility has been restricted only for students electing a noncomprehensive major that requires a minor, and then only slightly. "In addition, faculty and student opinion supports the conclusion that an overweening concern for flexibility often eventuates a degree program including the largest possible number of 'easy' courses."[18]

The authors conducted a survey of graduates during the summer of 1979, three years after implementing their new program. A number of open-ended questions allowed respondents to add to their answers on the otherwise structured questionnaire; 96 usable questionnaires were returned, representing a 15 percent response rate. Included were six questions to which respondents answered either yes or no or expressed a preference for the old or the new.

1. Did the program you were under prepare you well for business? Yes (89%) No (11%)

2. Does the new program provide an appropriate amount of flexibility for students in their programs? Yes (59%) No (41%)

3. Which program offers better preparation for life and eventual leadership in business? New (75%) Old (25%)

4. Which program offers greater practical application? New (72%) Old (28%)

5. Assuming that the new program offers students greater breadth, do you feel that this is beneficial or even necessary? Yes (85%) (No (15%)

6. Which program do you think would better prepare a person for dealing with choices and decisions to be made on the job? New (77%) (Old (23%)

The fact that only 15 percent of the sample contacted responded indicates that the results just quoted must be regarded with considerable caution, since those who do not respond in such forms of sampling are likely to feel hostile toward the entire situation, holding opinions that are not being measured. Furthermore, the responses were merely two-valued, not providing for a finer gradation of measurable responses. A response rate of at least 50 percent would have been much more desirable, with the responses being measured on Likert-type scales, which are sensitive to various degrees of opinion.

In summary, a number of issues have been especially prominent in the domain of business education. These include upgrading the overall quality of business students, achieving a better balance between vocational training and liberal arts general education, academic theory versus the practical needs for businessmen, communication and human relations skills versus purely technical knowledge, and the content of business administration curricula. Cayley and Harold criticize the typical core program as being too superficial in areas other than the area of concentration, instead suggesting their own program which goes into greater depth in many interrelated areas. The authors caution that flexibility must not be sacrificed on the altar of excessive structuring.

Meriting further discussion are these and other issues: modern management theory, competency-based instruction, student entrance requirements, the need for new emphases such as the quantitative curricula, the cooperative education development, and the concept of career development. These issues are taken up next.

MODERN MANAGEMENT THEORY

Business administration concerns more than merely standard business problems. They involve interaction with other individuals on a purely personal and social basis, therefore embracing the management of people. The business manager must, accordingly, deal with many of the same problems with which modern management theory concerns itself.

Modern managers must know how to deal with alienated workers characterized by a "lack of communication, poorly defined self-concept, apathy, lack of goals, resistance to change, and limited exercise of alternatives, choices and decisions."[19] Various means of reducing alienation are open to management. For example, the management structure of the chemical manufacturing unit of a large British enterprise was altered, simplifying and clarifying authority lines, increasing authority lines, increasing communication channels, and shortening the chains of command.

The results of this reorganization were improved
feelings of communication and knowledge and at
least a 5 percent increase in favorable attitudes toward work challenge and variety. Managers felt
that their work was worthwhile and meaningful;
they also felt that they had improved their standard
of living. [20]

Other solutions to management-employee problems include
getting to know and taking an interest in employees; giving workers
more job responsibility, more pay, and more fringe benefits; setting work-group goals, performance awards, full employment,
housing programs, national health insurance, higher educational
opportunities, retirement provisions, equalization of job amenities, freedom to rearrange tasks, union improvement and power,
training sessions, and effective education; and a change in job responsibility according to the needs of the particular employee. [21]
Robert Graham and Milton Valentine[22] observed that increasing
organizational size and complexity have usually been accompanied
by alienation but rejected so-called democratic management as an
ineffective solution. They suggested, instead, developing trust
through older employees capable of nurturing hope in junior employees. They also suggested adequate training that is not company dominated or too closely supervised and that recognizes the
importance of each individual.

Job stresses of many kinds can influence psychosocial life
and influence job satisfaction, emotional stability, performance,
and productivity negatively. Stress can be the result of role
ambiguity, qualitative or quantitative work overload or underload,
job insecurity, pressure deadlines, and responsibility for people.
According to the Work in America Institute, techniques are available to help individuals moderate the detrimental effects of occupational stress. "The best and probably the most complex and
expensive solution involves a major reorganization of working life
and personal value systems for millions of blue- and white-collar
workers."[23]

Some solutions are as simple as an alternative work sched-
ule that allows for flexible working hours (flexitime), permanent
part-time employment, and compressed workweeks. [24] Some
firms have reported achieving good results with programs that
train supervisors on the job. [25] Ridley J. Gros[26] cited research
emphasizing the fundamental role of the behavioral sciences and
communication skills in expediting management processes. Some

authorities recommend "work redesign" or job enrichment involving alteration of specific jobs (or systems of jobs) with the intent of improving both productivity and the quality of employee work experiences.[27]

Edgar H. Schein concluded that the personnel manager of the future must become a change agent, "one who will have to be much more oriented toward the organization as a whole, will have to be much more concerned about top management as his key client system, and will have to be much more oriented toward helping the organization to improve all of its management processes, not just those dealing with traditional personnel matters."[28] Schein cited a number of reasons underlying his conclusions: (1) the United States is in an age of rapid technological and social change; (2) the lifeblood of organizations consists of people and the relationships between them; (3) the more complex the organization, the more dependent it becomes on decisions made by the power centers usually at the top of the organization; (4) organizations are interlocking sets of formal and informal groups, not merely chains of authority relationships; (5) adaptive organizational change cannot occur without the help of change agents capable of viewing the entire organization as a dynamic system and determining where the key points are; and (6) behavioral science knowledge is essential in managing a change process.

The student of business administration should realize that successful management goes beyond mere technical competence in a specific area of professional responsibility. The foregoing discussion has indicated a number of specific variables and situations that the manager of people should be aware of, whether in business or any other kind of administration. However, unless the student has a convenient conceptual framework for summarizing the various aspects of modern management theory, there is the likelihood that understanding significant major concepts will be fragmented and applied in an ineffective, piecemeal manner. Accordingly, a number of fundamental concepts in modern management theory are worth learning. These fundamental concepts may be stated in terms of systems theory, action research, management by objectives, organization development, communication, creativity, and release of individual potential.

The Systems Concept

A major trend in almost all areas of administration has been the greater reliance on models of management science. One of these models is called systems thinking. General systems theory includes the man, the machine, and the total environment. It involves a collection of definitions, assumptions, and propositions that deal with reality as an integrated hierarchy of organizations of matter and energy. According to John A. Beckett, "These systems—not people—are the real managers, as we currently comprehend management."[29] Such systems are often intangible patterns of interrelationships and rules of behavior, so that formal as well as informal hierarchies must be included.

The systems concept aids the manager in better relating the subsystem to the whole. How an individual functions may well depend on adequately grasping the nature of the system in which performance is being judged.

However, systems thinking is largely a conceptual framework. By itself it cannot provide the specific technical knowledge required of management. Moreover, the presumably objective or scientific systems approach to freedom and purpose may be inadequate; science cannot manufacture value. The vital role played by pure power is well known. According to Beckett, "Systems thinking provides no answers to this issue, and again offers no value judgments."[30]

Action Research

Action research usually involves the participation of many persons in suggesting solutions to problems. Through total staff participation and feedback, the apparent and most likely methods for solving problems are looked into in detail. The criteria for an individual's or a group's performance are often decided in advance. Evaluation is not only normative (judging or rating the performers against some standard or norm of performance) but formative as well (evaluation for the purpose of improving performance).

Management by Objectives

Management by objectives (MBO) is a philosophy of management as well as a specific technique or skill. As a technique, it provides direction and purpose for every managerial act and allows greater discretionary powers to lower levels of management throughout the organization. As a humanistic philosophy, it converts institutional objectives into personal needs. Marie

DiVincenti sees MBO as a kind of supportive management. "Providing a supportive environment assures a maximum probability that each staff member, in the light of his background, values, desires and expectations, will view each experience and interaction as supportive—as something which builds and maintains his sense of personal worth and importance."[31]

At the upper management levels, objectives are typically determined after an examination of resources, market position, opportunities, and managerial capabilities. These objectives are accepted and implementation strategies decided on. Each level provides objectives for the next lower level of management, but allows lower levels to participate in the objective formation process within prescribed limits. Douglas C. Basil is of the opinion that the MBO approach "prevents the side-tracking of management and managerial resources into courses of action that are not in accord with corporate long-range objectives."[32]

Involvement in the setting of objectives is also a motivational technique, since individual commitments and accomplishments lead to more satisfaction. The use of objectives provides standards of performance against which to appraise management. The manager's performance in realizing the objective is a realistic and measurable means by which his ability and worth to the organization may be determined.

As a consequence of employee involvement, participation, and sharing of objectives, employees come to direct their efforts toward organizational goals as a means of achieving their own needs and objectives. MBO assumes that people exercise self-direction and self-control in relation to goals to which they are personally committed. Achieving mutual goals becomes of primary importance to them.

Ideally, MBO contrasts with management by control. MBO requires a participative approach in which organizational conditions are arranged so that people can achieve their own goals by directing their efforts toward the goals of the organization within which they are working. It is the job of management to provide opportunities and remove obstacles in a way that will encourage growth and release individual potential.

Organization Development

Organization Development (OD) is a term that denotes a planned, managed, systematic process designed to change the

culture, systems, and behavior of an organization in order to improve the organization's effectiveness in solving its problems and
achieving its objectives. The emphasis is on interaction and be-
haviors, that is, "the technical resources are interrelated with the
human resources."[33] The objective is to maximize the efficiency
of the technical system within the constraints of the social system
and vice versa.

OD seeks to modify behavioral patterns on a group problem-
solving basis. A key question is, How can a quality of life be
created and maintained within the organization so that employees
"produce valid and useful information especially about their more
important problems, make effective decisions, and generate a high
degree of human energy and commitment to their decisions in
order to diligently monitor and effectively implement them"?[34]
The individual may be developed within the context of the group or
within the context of the organization. Typical activities in OD
include attitude measurement, diagnostic interviewing, problem
solving, goal setting, communication improvement, conflict reso-
lution, task force utilization, job design, and evaluation and
measurement of effectiveness.

Three important activities in OD are diagnosis, planning for
change, and interventions. Once ineffective functioning is perceived, the first step toward treatment is diagnosis. Diagnosis
may involve analysis of the organizational structure to see if it
can and should be realigned. It may involve studying the communications channels and flow of information to see where and for
what reasons they break down. Diagnosis may also be a more
complex process of surveying the organization to determine the
attitudes that block free and open communication. OD specialists
may interview individuals and groups to pinpoint the source or
underlying causes of the problem.

Diagnostic data are analyzed, digested, and interpreted before being fed back to the organization. In some instances, the
diagnosis is fed back only to the management members sponsoring
the diagnosis; more often it is presented to groups having the
problem in order that they can use the information during the next
stage, the development of strategies for change.

Once the diagnostic data have been gathered, analyzed, and
fed back, the organization should then develop a plan to deal with
the cause of poor organizational functioning. Participation in
strategic planning may be extended to include nonmanagerial employees who are affected by the activities being planned. Typically, there is a specification of the action that is to be taken,

who is responsible for the action, what the timing will be, and who in the organization is to be the client for the action. Ideally, there should be some provision for evaluating the effectiveness of the action. According to Chris Argyris, the primary tasks of intervention are the following:

1. Generating and helping the organization to generate valid information, which they can understand, about their problems;

2. Creating opportunities for the organization to search effectively for solutions to their problems; and

3. Creating conditions for internal commitment to these choices and to the apparatus for the continual monitoring of the action taken.[35]

Interventions may be in the nature of social intervention, administrative intervention, or technical intervention. Measurement and evaluation are useful for determining whether the diagnosis was an accurate one and whether the interventions accomplished what they were intended to accomplish.

One may at this point be quite impressed with all this machinery and wonder why management should ever have any problems if they have at their fingertips such wisdom. To begin with, one major obstacle has already been mentioned, namely, that science cannot manufacture value. Furthermore, it is a gratuitous assumption that individual and organization goals of necessity should be congruent or even that they can be made congruent. It is not at all clear that institutional objectives can always be converted into personal needs as some writers on the subject seem to assume. An organization that is polluting the environment or carrying out "shady" deals of dubious ethical variety is not necessarily of the kind with which employees should identify their own aspirations.

Given a tolerable level of organizational ethics and social management purpose, techniques such as action research, MBO, and OD constitute a conceptual framework useful in approaching management problems. Communication, creativity, and release of individual potential relate directly to the kinds of processes that such a conceptual framework implies.

Communication and Creativity

There is much similarity between organization development and such concepts as systems thinking, action research, and management by objectives. Fundamental to all these areas is communication, since the assignment of responsibilities and the perceptions that individuals have of their jobs will ultimately depend on a good communication process. According to Paul Mali, the objective-setting process will depend on a process that requires efficient communication.[36] Individual effectiveness and understanding of work and teamwork responsibilities are based on insight and understanding that derive from good communication processes.

Yet, experts concur that there is much confusion in the field of communications. A major problem is that the communication process can easily deteriorate into a one-directional, downward flow. Despite an executive's various skills, to get a job done requires reliance on other people to do it for him; this means communicating with them. Frank E. Fischer and Lydia Strong identify an "X factor" in the manager's job as the extra skill inherent in all his activities, a factor whose presence means the difference between success and failure.[37] The X factor is communication.

The need for managerial and employee input at all levels will in the final analysis depend on a kind of creative listening. According to William F. Keefe, there is too much talking down or out and not enough receiving up through listening. He feels that, with authority flowing out or down and little or no ideation or information flowing in and up, creative voices are silenced. "Where authority functions in an atmosphere of inadequate communication, it may actually arouse resistance to its orders and decrees."[38]

The Release of Individual Potential

Some observers hold that managers in business fail to develop their personnel not because of a lack of interest or want of trying. The problem is seen as one in which the process of developing people is separated from the everyday running of the business. According to Guy B. Ford, "instead of building growth into the job, we put our personnel man in charge of employee development, and in so doing we take a prime responsibility from the line officer and give the personnel manager an assignment that tends toward the impossible and, at best, is frustrating."[39]

A merely supportive attitude by management is not enough to foster release of individual potential through personal growth on the job. Special effort, ingenuity, and tact are essential. Academic discussions, such as those that argue whether personnel administration is a profession or an art, tend toward a jargon unintelligible to those outside the field and to many within it. According to Ford, a manager "might better apply himself to helping each line officer be more effective in his job."[40]

Many thinkers on management believe that participation programs are likely to release individual potential more than pressure-oriented, threatening, or punitive management approaches. It is claimed that participative programs will increase productivity, as well as improve loyalty, attitudes, interest, and involvement in work. Participation programs are more likely than various other programs to result in satisfying the goals of both the organization and the employee.

MANAGING THE NEW GENERATION

It has been said by some that most members of the new generation resist constant, close supervision. Some have likened the problem to the widening gap between generations. However, some writers see nothing in this to cause alarm. Thomas F. Stroh finds the new generation superior and more knowledgeable than prior generations; their impatience and suspicion is not surprising. His solution consists partly in the establishing of a more sophisticated version of management techniques in which the subordinate and manager together agree on goals and criteria for performance by an individual or group. This participation in determining on what basis efforts will be judged and this involvement of followers in the planning process "will increase their commitment to the goals and objectives which are established."[41]

Peter F. Drucker sees management as a social function, one that helps shape culture and society. His concern goes much deeper than mere organizational effectiveness and efficiency for its own sake. Drucker rejects such slogans as "Everybody should do his own thing" and "Down with organization!" He holds that society cannot do without services that only certain institutions can provide. These institutions must perform responsibly, even though in an autonomous manner. Unless strong, performing autonomous institutions are preserved, the alternative is tyranny. According to Drucker, tyranny substitutes one absolute boss for the pluralism of competing institutions.

It substitutes terror for responsibility. It does indeed do away with the institutions, but only by submerging all of them in the one all-embracing bureaucracy of the apparat. It does produce goods and services, though only fitfully, wastefully at a low level, and at an enormous cost in suffering, humiliation, and frustration. To make our institutions perform responsibly, autonomously, and on a high level of achievement is thus the only safeguard of freedom and dignity in the pluralist society of institutions.[42]

PARTICIPATION

Some observers point to other cultures, note the absence of certain problems, and then suggest that we study their techniques and apply them to the U.S. scene. Theoretically, this is plausible; practically, cultural differences are usually so powerful that management methodology cannot overcome them.

For example, the methods of Japanese management have attracted considerable attention in the international business community. The Japanese business world did amazingly well not only before but during the mid-1970s recession. A major reason for this has to do with the intricate structure that governs the practices of labor and industry, namely, the "humanistic" management methods practiced by Japanese management, especially with regard to participation of the work force in management decisions.

However, these practices do not exist in a cultural vacuum. The main features of Japanese management originate from social customs, attitudes, and mores deeply engrained in the Japanese people for thousands of years. Any technique taken out of the Japanese cultural context may fail if put into a different cultural context. Therefore, U.S. management will have to work out its own theories relevant to its own culture, borrowing whatever can be realistically and profitably adapted.

U.S. culture has a number of inherent obstacles to successful participation management not found in other cultures such as the Japanese. According to Jerome S. Rosow, "these obstacles are deep-seated and represent a combination of historical, psychological, and economic factors."[43] He lists seven serious obstacles as follows:

1. Managerial philosophy generally considers worker participation of limited value at any level in the organization. The predominant belief is that costs outweigh the benefits.

2. Because the art of participative management is new, top executives lack experience and know-how in dealing with it.

3. The concept is viewed by executives, managers, and supervisors as a threat in terms of conventional power and authority. The problems of managing an increased conflict of ideas and sharing power are frightening to many.

4. Impatience to achieve short-term economic gains while dealing with a sensitive new process that requires long-term commitments forecasts at best an uneven pathway to meaningful results.

5. Unions are suspicious of the process and fear that it will weaken the adversary relationship, complicate the current problems of collective bargaining, and impose new problems for their memberships.

6. There is a shortage of talented third parties who can engender the necessary trust and provide the required know-how to introduce and maintain a participative style of working.

7. Broad-based participation threatens the framework of conventional, hierarchical organizations and is seen as topsy-turvey management, which may substitute consensus decision making for one-man rule.

Rosow cites a number of economic and sociological factors operant in the United States today that indicate the possibility of more future participation by employees in the management scene. He states them as follows:

1. The permissive society has fostered a change in authority roles. Employees have higher expectations and place intelligent limits on the exercise of authority over their lives.

2. The decline in confidence in business, government, education, and other major institutions has affected employees who are members of such organizations. The relative decline in trust and confidence weakens performance on the job.

3. Changing attitudes toward religion and work reflect the values of a postreligious society that no longer views work as a punishment that will be rewarded in the afterlife.

4. Less commitment to the work ethic and greater public cynicism have spread to all classes of workers: blue-collar, white-collar, professional, managerial, and executive.

5. The era of rising entitlements has created a widespread feeling that jobs, income, employee benefits, and a higher standard of living are no longer privileges but rights.

6. Employee expectations for participation in decisions affecting their jobs have reached the point at which a majority consider this a right. Among younger workers, 62 percent expressed this view in 1977.

7. Significant changes in Japan and Western Europe teach us that young U.S. workers are not a peculiar breed and that, for the first time, work must compete with other personal values.

8. The rising educational level of workers, combined with higher costs per employee, creates an economic necessity to secure a better return on the human investment.

9. Growing automation and advanced technology in both office and factory increase the complexity of the interaction between man and machine.

10. Changes in U.S. social values, mores, and folkways have been rapid and penetrating over the past decade. By contrast, large organizations are slow to change. Thus, the institutional lag persists and must be corrected over the decade ahead to bring organizational life into a more harmonious balance with society and its values.

In short, there is the dilemma of a very highly expensive and highly educated work force whose productivity is declining.

DEMOCRACY AT WORK

According to Rosow, the modern organization is a total society in a microcosm in which employees hold voluntary membership. The U.S. worker expects working conditions to reflect the political and social conditions in other areas of life. For example, U.S. clerical and hourly workers feel that they are not treated fairly, not respected as individuals, and not listened to.

Part of this is due, according to Rosow, to many of the current working population being products of a permissive and affluent society, with expectations and a sense of entitlement rising faster than the performance of most work institutions. There is an increasing tendency to question authority; employees expect a more open and interactive workplace environment that resembles their life-styles in other areas. Rosow's reaction to this is a suggestion of new strategies and new policies, a new style of supervision that will involve less autocracy and more skill in managing dissent, a style reflecting a patience and willingness to expose power to criticism without unreasonable fear of loss of control. The issue for Rosow seems to involve the pure technology of group leadership rather than ethical or moral factors, with general psychology taking precedence over moral arguments.

Yet, when Rosow turns his attention to corporations, he openly challenges their selfishness and lack of responsibility. One may likewise apply such arguments to employee ranks. Ethics involve a concern for others, not just some abstract legalistic, moral, or boy scout code. It would seem that Rosow's rather penetrating analysis of the scene points to psychological elements in the U.S. worker that are selfish, far more so than for the Japanese worker, who is willing to sacrifice for the good of the organization.

Complex issues involving quality of work life should not be oversimplified to a single issue such as cooperation and responsibility. It is precisely such an important issue that will be obscured through a purely technical analysis. Perhaps further cross-cultural studies and experience will more fully bring out the importance of attitude and work ethics as fundamental causes of modern management problems in the United States.

COMPETENCY-BASED INSTRUCTION

Accountability in education has become an increasingly widespread concept in U.S. society. Ever since the competency-based teacher education movement was started in the late 1960s, there has been considerable debate over the title, objectives, responsibility, and control of teacher education. B. Bertha Wakin reported on the recommendations of a special task group at the State University of New York at Albany. The task group concluded that, in addition to the general competencies needed by all teachers, business teachers needed to meet the following additional performance objectives:

1. The business teacher demonstrates a critical understanding and appreciation of the American economic system.

2. The business teacher functions effectively as a person within the business environment.

3. The business teacher evinces an awareness of job opportunities in business occupations in both the private and public sectors including beginning

jobs and promotional opportunities as they are
and as they are likely to be in the future.

4.   The business teacher effectively fits students for
a variety of business occupations including beginning jobs and advancement opportunities.

5.   The business teacher prepares students to act
effectively and intelligently as consumers of
business goods and services.

6.   The business teacher takes definite steps to
keep up-to-date on changing conditions in business employment and business practices.

In addition to these objectives, Wakin contended that the four
following competencies were needed:

1.   The business teacher develops a curriculum
providing those experiences which prepare students both to enter business occupations and
to live effectively as consumers of business
goods and services.

2.   The business teacher develops standards of
achievement (cooperatively) which are consistent with the abilities of students and with
the requirements of the occupations for which
they are preparing.

3.   The business teacher uses appropriate methods
of teaching in developing the desirable general
skills, knowledges, understandings, apprecia-
tions, and attitudes as well as those characteristics which are peculiar to business situations.

4.   The business teacher uses appropriate instruments,
devices, and processes to measure progress of
students toward realistic occupational standards
and toward the achievement of abilities to operate
as intelligent consumers.[44]

John E. Graham singled out the use of competency-based accounting instruction as a means of adapting business education to
individual differences among students. "A unit of a traditional
class of accounting principles or bookkeeping was reorganized in

an effort to develop each student to his fullest potential through the design and implementation of an individualized competency-based learning system."[45] In such an approach, time becomes a very flexible element. More important are both the specification of learning goals in measurable terms and the requirement that the learner effect observable behavior changes in knowledge and/or skills, demonstrating a competence before proceeding to more complex goals. In short, Graham recommended thorough mastery of skills at the individual's own pace.

Graham's treatment of an accounting-principles unit in the context of individualized competency-based learning is highly instructive. After students participate in the preliminary instructional activity for the accounting lesson, they are required to complete some form of evaluation to determine whether or not certain skills have been acquired. These evaluative (criterion-referenced) tests are administered in the form of a problem, an exercise, or an objective type question. In many instances, the student merely submits problems or exercises that have been completed as part of the learning activities. The instructor keeps a record of individually completed activities. This record enables the instructor to know at all times what activities the student has successfully completed for every lesson.

If the instructor decides that the lesson performance is acceptable, the student goes on to the next lesson in the module. If the lesson performance is not acceptable, the instructor diagnoses the situation and prescribes alternative instructional activities. These activities are intended to prepare the student to once again take the evaluative tests. The student is continually recycled in this way until there is evidence that the lesson objectives have been mastered.

In applying this approach, Graham found that the fastest student was able to complete the materials and attain mastery for a complete module five days sooner than the slower students. However, the results showed that students who possess different individual characteristics can achieve at a stated competency level if they are given appropriate materials and sufficient time to master them. The diversity of individual differences depends on more than just general intelligence. Prior business experience, years of high school bookkeeping, previous accounting instruction pretest scores, and time available to complete a unit all enter into the picture.

Graham indicated that how well a student performs at the end of a unit may provide misleading evidence unless a comparison is made with the initial performance. For example, some students with high terminal performance scores may have gained very little from the instruction because their beginning scores were also high.

Probably the best evaluation of Graham's approach may be found in student commentaries. According to one student, "I think it is easier to learn this way because if you don't understand something the first time, you can stay with one problem until you understand it without getting behind."[46]

STUDENT ENTRANCE REQUIREMENTS

A major problem swirling around student entrance requirements is the challenge of satisfying students with widely different needs, abilities, and backgrounds. According to Joseph P. Giusti and George R. Lovette, "If the business school continues to adapt its programs to meet the differences of incoming students as well as the fluid demands of society, the business school could very well be at the commencement of its greatest period of expansion and public service."[47]

Higher education institutions are becoming increasingly complex and their students more heterogeneous. Accordingly, a student development concept becomes an attempt to solve the inevitable conflict between these two trends. David T. Borland pointed out the need for a "process to implement organizationally a reduction of the consequences resulting from the daily interface between students and 'the system.' "[48]

According to Borland, those in higher education tend to jump on the bandwagon of the latest educational fad without adequate preliminary examination or bothering to find out where the bandwagon is going. Analysis before action is crucial, and neglect of it for reasons of time or costs can be wasteful in the long run. "We do not do our homework and we end up with an expensive trip whose destination is not where we ought to have been heading."[49]

It is not surprising, then, that a cynicism naturally arises about colleges and universities and their ability to change systems. Without knowing organizational contingencies, change is difficult to effect. Borland sees organizational power as a major factor instrumental in overcoming resistance to change; implementation of student development programs will require the analysis of organizational power systems.

Analysis of organizational power systems, according to Borland, should include a description of operational goals and

objectives on a particular campus. Available resources and potential barriers to student development goals must be identified,
especially in relation to relevant power sources. "An implementation plan of strategies and tactics must be formulated which will
overcome institutional barriers and will link resources and power
together supported by a contingent intrinsic and extrinsic rewards
system."[50]

If special provision is made for the identification and placement of nontraditional students, entrance requirements need not,
generally, cause great concern. Laurence A. Brown, reporting
on the experience of the University of Mid-America (UMA), mentioned a multimedia course employing an integral television component and using special UMA Accounting I materials.[51] A major
conclusion of the study was that nontraditional adult learners who
completed the multimedia course could be expected to achieve as
well or better than on-campus learners using the same course
materials within a more traditional college course structure. This
conclusion was interpreted as one that would help allay fears of
external audiences that UMA courses are not as rigorous as on-
campus courses. "In the light of the open admissions policy of
UMA and the common enrollment of adults not recently involved in
academic pursuits and/or without college experience, this conclusion, though tentative, is gratifying."[52]

Other conclusions of the Brown report are worth noting. The
nontraditional learners rated the multimedia course as more appealing than did on-campus students. The use of an integral television component of a multimedia, nontraditional course had no
significant effect on either achievement or course appeal with on-
campus students. It had been anticipated that the nontraditional
course would be more appealing, but such was not the case. There
was no significant difference detected between the appeal of a multimedia, nontraditional course and the appeal of a traditional college course when two groups of similar on-campus students were
compared. Evidently, the use of television had no magic effect
that some audiovisual buffs would have others believe.

Joel Podell, Abraham Axelrod, Jonas Falik, and Dennis
Green emphasized the importance of the introductory college business course at Queensborough Community College at Bayside, New
York. The purpose of this course is to provide students with an
overview of business and to assist them in choosing a particular
area of concentration within the business curriculum. This objective has necessitated creating a learning environment that enables
the maximum number of students to achieve their goals. "This has

required a revamping of our approach to the course and a change in the teaching methodologies utilized. "[53] Emphasis is not only on the standard academic content but also on the dynamic nature of the actual business world. Learning is enhanced by focusing on the student's own experience.

For example, the debate-type format may be used in order to foster a higher degree of student involvement in the learning process. The students are thereby provided with an opportunity to develop their skills in researching an issue and develop an appreciation for the importance of singling out the essential elements of an issue. Podell feels that a special kind of debate especially suitable for the introductory business course is a labor-management negotiating session. The realism thus introduced is rarely achieved in the average classroom setting.

> Eight volunteers from the class are presented with a hypothetical case and are expected to negotiate a labor contract. Four students assume the role of union negotiators while the other four represent management. Each side is expected to meet twice outside of class, with the instructor, in order to devise its negotiating strategy. The actual negotiating session takes place in class with both sides sitting around the bargaining table discussing (often vehemently) the merits of their respective positions. The only ground rule set by the instructor is that a settlement must be reached on all matters (wages, pensions, and a health insurance plan) within one period. The remainder of the class is expected to appraise the reasonableness of the settlement arrived at in the negotiating session.[54]

Podell indicates that such an activity invariable receives the enthusiastic support of the students. The students feel that they have acquired genuine understanding of what actually happens around a negotiating table in a real-world setting.

Marguerite E. Donovan of the College of Saint Rose at Albany, New York, discussed the problem of accepting or rejecting transfer students and reporting on them to prospective employers. The college devised special courses in the area of business/ economics and behavioral science in business. As a result, the faculty came to know the students better than they did otherwise. The Business and Media course, in particular, gave students an opportunity to acquire experience and confidence in listening and observing effectively; following directions; recording events accurately; thinking and speaking logically, professionally, and correctly; and dictating, all within the framework of the business situation.[55]

QUANTITATIVE CURRICULA

While few, if any, authorities challenge the typical business student's need for quantititative knowledge, there is some disagreement as to how much and exactly what kind of such knowledge is required. In 1961, John M. Kuhlman argued that business schools were not preparing students adequately in the field of quantitative analysis.[56] A 1972 study by Roger L. Burford and Donald R. Williams[57] noted the increasing emphasis on quantitative requirements. A 1977 study by James C. Van Pelt and Edwin C. Spencer confirmed the Burford-Williams finding of considerable diversity in the structure of quantitative programs, as well as of variations in the departmental location of such programs.[58] Van Pelt and Spencer believe that today's business schools are placing significant emphasis on their quantitative curricula.

The increasing complexity of society has intensified the requirement for more relevant information on a more timely basis. This need has created a demand for systems analysis using quantitative methods, especially in combination with computer technology. Daryl Nord and Tom Seymour make a sharp distinction between the computer science needs of the business school student and of the graduate in computer science. The most common names used for data processing in the school of business are these: information systems and operational research, information systems, management science, business data processing, and administrative services.

A business data processing graduate has a strong background in the functional parts of a business organization while a computer science major may not. A business data processing person learns how to use mathematical models compared to a computer science person who develops a math model. Both graduates are usually able to program in several different computer languages. A computer science

> student usually understands the complete structure
> of the computer versus the business student who
> understands the business organizational structure.[59]

Properly organized and well-taught quantitative programs consider these and other distinctions carefully.

The Van Pelt and Spencer study mentioned earlier provides some relevant details regarding the quantitative curricula of various accredited undergraduate business schools. Representatives from 80 schools responded to a questionnaire mailed to 150 business schools with undergraduate American Assembly of Collegiate Schools of Business (AACSB) accreditations. The responses indicated the structure and content of required quantitative courses. All 80 respondents listed statistics courses and 74 listed mathematics foundations courses as core requirements. Statistics was taught mainly within the business schools whereas the mathematics foundations courses were taught in departments outside the business schools. More than two-thirds of the schools required decision-science type courses, and these were taught in the business school without exception. Only 12 schools taught a mathematics-of-finance-type course as a separate subject, although some topics under that heading were taught in other courses.

For decision-science and mathematics-of-finance courses, those given three semester hours of credit predominated. On the average, about twelve semester hours in the quantitative area were required. However, the range of total semester hour, quantitative requirements varied considerably, thus indicating considerable variation in the structure and emphasis given quantitative programs. The subjects receiving the most emphasis were discrete probability distributions and linear regression (statistics), linear programming—primal (decision science), differential calculus (mathematical foundations), and compound interest and discount (mathematics of finance).

COOPERATIVE EDUCATION

The National Commission for Cooperative Education has defined cooperative education as

> a working partnership in which an educational institution joins with an employer in a structured relationship. Its basic purpose is that of providing a

> means whereby a student can combine study at the
> institution with a work experience which is under
> the supervision of the employer.[60]

Cooperative programs have grown rapidly only in recent years, although the very first such program in higher education was started at the University of Cincinnati in 1906. Few of today's programs operate in yesteryear's fashion. Joe Thomas sampled almost 200 colleges and universities with such programs and found that a majority of the programs is elective; business and non-business majors alike are placed by an office or individual specifically responsible for placing cooperative students; most institutions regularly involve teaching faculty members in supervising students, with a few schools limiting the number of students whom a given faculty member may supervise; and more than four-fifths of the institutions in question allow academic credit for such experience. The most common problems encountered are locating enough students for such programs, mossbacked faculty resistance, and insufficient administrative support. "Results of this survey do not show a single 'best' way to operate a co-op program."[61]

In a survey of attitudes toward cooperative education, Christopher G. L. Pratt contacted 93 members of the higher education community using an instrument consisting of 19 attitudinal statements. The study sample agreed that cooperative education is a valid instructional method exposing students to a unique corpus of knowledge. It helps them to establish and achieve behavioral and operational objectives and test values and to develop skills offering them sound technical training and a concomitant vocabulary. "However, they significantly differed in opinion that students in these programs attain unique competencies or that cooperative education is a valid approach to learning."[62] There was major disagreement between cooperative education professionals and faculty members, with the latter generally not supporting the idea that cooperative experience is a valid academic approach to learning. "Co-op personnel and teaching faculty often concur on the values which accrue to students participating in Co-op, but frequently they do not agree on the full academic character of Cooperative Education."[63]

Making higher education responsive to the needs of the real business world remains a serious problem. The relevance of collegiate business education to the demonstrated and anticipated needs of the business community has been questioned widely. Gerard E. Nistal cites a Carnegie Foundation finding seemingly supporting the need for cooperative education, "MBA students are currently being trained in top level problem analysis and managerial decision making, and thus expect such assignments on their first job; while business firms expect them to start as paraprofessionals and learn the business from the ground up before being delegated such responsibility and authority."[64] Furthermore, according to the foundation, students are increasingly demanding a real-world pragmatism and relevance in their curricula and syllabi so as to provide them with marketable skills. Such practical experience is also fundamental in educational psychology, where theory and practice combine to create a sound learning approach.

Richard Dieffenderfer, Lee Kopp, and Orest Cap have provided an excellent resource handbook for improving vocational teacher education linkage with business, industry, and labor. The handbook has three main objectives.

1. To identify various types and sources of information appropriate to the business, industry, and labor interests of vocational teacher education departments.
2. To describe for vocational teacher educators appropriate ways to access and utilize selected business, industry, and labor information resources.
3. To organize and present resource information in a way encouraging its use in meeting the business, industry, and labor-linkage objectives of vocational teacher education departments.

Eight topics are featured in the handbook: staff development, advisory committees, cooperative internships, personnel exchange programs, workshops, site visits, resource persons, and program support.[65]

Another reason for offering cooperative education is the realization that "too many schools and colleges fall short in providing adequate and/or current programs because the changing needs of industry are not taken into account."[66] Students frequently discover that what they have learned is not what industry needs, or that it is no longer relevant. Rall and O'Brien tried to formulate methods and procedures for job identification and placement based on industrial needs. Their objective was to pinpoint common needs in curriculum industries (those employing students trained in a specific technology or vocation) by using procedures involving a sufficiently large representation of such industries. A significant trend in line with this purpose is adapting and changing college curricula continually to meet changing job requirements.

Distributive education (DE) programs have been an important aspect of cooperative education since the George-Deen Act, passed by Congress in 1936, legitimatized such programs. The Vocational Education Act of 1963 introduced further changes. Prior to 1963, distributive education programs consisted of either in-school classes for youth who were 16 years of age or older with the co-operative plan as the program of administration or part-time classes to instruct adults employed in distribution.

Enactment of the 1963 statute produced a number of changes. There had previously been no instructional programs for unem-ployed youth and adults, no program administration employing the project plan, no specific percentage of total funding to be allocated for research, and no encouragement for providing programs for special needs groups. The 1963 act corrected these deficiencies. Later on, the Vocational Education Amendments of 1968 mandated that the various states offer programs to meet the special needs of groups outside the mainstream of public education. The National Advisory Council for Vocational Education and the allocation of monies for the various state advisory councils for vocational edu-cation provided a means of monitoring results as well as propos-ing areas for further development.

Historically, distributive education evolved from retailing education. Many consider DE to be retailing despite the great variety of courses ranging from advertising service to broadcast-ing and the performing arts. Some mistakenly conclude that the distributive program deals only with entry-level positions such as salespeople, cashiers, and stock clerks. "In reality, the whole range of positions in a retailing enterprise are viable positions for which a student might aspire and thus be prepared in an instruc-tional program."[67] Marketing includes the distributive functions of selling, sales promotion, buying, operations, market research, and management. Marketing is the nucleus around which the other areas of instruction are focused.

As in other areas of cooperative education, competency-based instruction in DE can provide a basis for vocational realism and accountability. Training plans are crucial. Their actual use at the local level is often skimpy and sometimes merely a facade. Reasons for this vary. Some claim that teachers have neither the time nor the professional background or that employers do not want to devote that much time to the process of developing and following the plan.

This is regrettable because research findings indicate that employers who use training plans perceive the cooperative distributive education student to be in a training environment as opposed to co-op DE students without training plans. It seems clear that the employer views the use of the training plan in the distributive education program as a way to prepare youth and adults for entry-level employment and advancement in the field of distribution and not merely as a work-study program. [68]

CAREER DEVELOPMENT

An important development has recently occurred in U.S. career education. Federal funding for career training and counseling increased from $9 million in 1971 to nearly $70 million in 1977. [69] Foundations and corporations have also supported career education, with numerous high schools and colleges adding practical courses to their curricula. Reasons for these increases are multiple. Clifton R. Wharton contends the following:

1. To an ever increasing extent, people are categorizing the content of college courses as removed from and irrelevant to the world of work;

2. People believe that such career education as does exist is misdirected—that colleges are, for instance, training too many teachers and too few electronic technicians;

3. Unemployment among young people has increased, partly because they have not been trained for existing jobs;

4. A few scholars are spreading the idea that today's students are being overeducated—humane learning and science is preparing them to become leaders rather than technicians or service workers; and

5. Hard times—a slowed economic growth, inflation, and high taxes—are ahead for the United States and people need to return to the basics, to do-it-yourself, to the ethic of hard work. [70]

Traditional work values held that women did not need to work if they could possibly avoid doing so; the man as sole breadwinner could thereby buttress his own self-esteem; money and status were sufficient to motivate most people; loyalty to the employing organization was fundamental; identity was achieved through the work role; and that "a job was defined as a paid activity that provided steady full-time work to the male breadwinner with compensation adequate to provide at least the necessities, and, with luck, some luxuries, for an intact nuclear family."[71]

New values are changing these views. Leisure is becoming more important and jobs are less satisfying for men, with a paying job becoming a status symbol of greater importance to women. Many of today's workers do not find self-fulfillment in their job or job status. "The New Breed person demands that his or her individuality be recognized."[72] A better educated work force is refusing to accept the former alienations that have inhered in society and still do.

> One thing that organizations can do, in response, is to pay more attention to the needs of their employees. If they want to make the most of their human resources, they had better understand the new job values—and start thinking of ways to improve the quality of work.[73]

The changing role of women in the work world reflects a number of historical trends. The industrial revolution in Western society brought with it a radical separation of work and family roles. This resulted in the consolidation of work under the control of men; women were identified with the home and child care. However, sex roles gradually became more egalitarian, and there emerged a tendency for married women to reenter the labor force while still young. Social and technological developments helped free women to pursue other than their traditional roles. The movement of women into the labor force had a sharp influence on the structure of the family.

A family is really a collection of interrelated roles. The wife's role is typically involved with such variables as housekeeping, child care, sex, recreation, and others. Satisfaction in these roles, especially where both the husband and wife pursue a career, may be subject to strain. A high degree of commitment is essential to maintain a stable family structure where both spouses work in the sense of pursuing a vocation or job outside the home.

Thus, employment status for women has required a radical change in their pattern of activities, commitments, and responsibilities. The consequent change in women's roles has in turn caused strain in the traditional family structure. Sources of stress stem from such dilemmas as work overload, role conflict, and discrepancies between personal and social norms.

Women's liberation is not the only indicator of changing commitment in the work force. New attitudes and views have emerged to challenge the old work ethic. According to Roger E. Calhoun, an old joke is being revived in organizations. One executive asks another, "How many people work in your organization?" and the other replies, "About half."[74]

Few observers doubt that there is sluggish productivity in the United States, that the nation faces a weakening of productivity growth. Productivity in the United States has not kept pace with growth in foreign nations. Calhoun believes that workers of Japan, for instance, are motivated by a strong work ethic. Collectively, they are prepared to work harder and keep goods flowing abroad. In Japan and other countries workers are evidently prepared to make sacrifices where U.S. workers are not.

The problem is not just one of attitude or work ethic alone. Calhoun indicates that part of the problem involves lack of skills and training. It is difficult to hire people who fully understand their jobs beforehand. Because workers' attitudes and skills have a significant impact on their productivity, training and development must be expanded and become part of business costs. Better personnel practices can improve attitudes, and better training can improve skills. "And, if workers have the right attitudes and the right skills we have every right to expect improvements in productivity."[75]

In recent years, the relationship between postsecondary school education and careers has become increasingly discordant rather than concordant.

> Higher education has become a disaster area for a
> large number of reasons traceable to the educational
> institutions themselves; to irrational dependence on
> our inherited frontier ideology and laissez-faire pol-
> icy in respect not only to our economy but also in
> respect to the social and political orders; and to the
> growing erratic and uncoordinated role of govern-
> ment.[76]

Hauser discerns an imperative need to reexamine the role of higher education in the light of the needs of contemporary and anticipated situations. In particular, more integration is needed between education and the world of work, and education ought to become a lifelong process. Hauser maintains that curricula should be modified to incorporate training in salable skills, as well as providing a liberal education. Career counseling and guidance should be utilized to a great extent, with the close integration of such services with curriculum planning and implementation. Hauser rejects the traditional conflict between a liberal education and training for work, favoring a whole individual conversant with both.

The following definition of career education, provided by the National Advisory Council for Career Education, summarizes many of the issues involved in career education: Career education is a person-centered, developmental, deliberate, and collaborative effort by educators, parents, and business-industry-labor-government personnel systematically to promote the career development of all persons by creating experiences to help them learn academic, vocational, and basic skills; achieve a sense of agency in making informed career decisions; and master the developmental tasks facing them at various life stages through curriculum, counseling, and community.[77]

Lorraine S. Hansen also provides definitions of career development and career guidance, both necessary adjuncts to career education. According to Hansen, career development is a continuous, life-long, person-centered process of developmental experiences focused on seeking, obtaining, and processing information about self (values, interests, abilities); occupational-educational alternatives; life-style and role options; and socioeconomic and labor market trends. It engages in purposeful planning in order to make reasoned decisions about work and its relation to other life roles with benefit to self and society. Hansen defines career guidance as a systematic program involving counselors and teachers in a career education program designed to increase knowledge of self, occupations, training paths, and life-styles; labor market trends and employability skills; and the career decision-making process. It helps the individual gain self-direction through purposefully and consciously integrating work, family, leisure, and community roles.

Harvard University President Derek Bok has asserted that no business school today is adequate in meeting the problems facing new graduates as they enter the corporate world. The increasing diversification of firms and their increasing penetration into foreign markets has generated new problems. In addition to established problems such as changes in consumer taste, technological advances, competitive behavior, and aggregate demand, graduates must now deal with Organization of Petroleum Exporting Countries decisions, changing economic policies, and even foreign coups. Another problem that schools must now recognize is that human problems have intensified "as different groups of employees have begun to challenge established hierarchies and traditional ways of doing business."[78]

Career education for business schools must be relevant to specific situations of the most varied sort. For instance, Claus Reschke points to the need for better foreign-language preparation for those students who will be performing their duties in foreign countries. He proposes a 12-month, semiintensive language program based on a combination of well-tested and innovative methods in language instruction. "These include a modular approach to the teaching of social-linguistic situations, culture, and the basic vocabulary essential to each student's professional area . . . with an eight-to-twelve week practicum in the student's professional field in the target language country."[79]

Consistent with new trends in career development is IBM's emphasis on rewarding managers for "people development." Over the past six or seven years, all managers with the exception of the older, first-level supervisors have participated in a career development workshop. The goal of this workshop is to help managers learn how to develop their subordinates through awareness of topics such as appraisal and counseling, recognition, equal opportunity, career development, technical vitality, communication, delegation, leadership and maturation, staffing, and sensitivity.[80]

Ralph W. Tyler emphasizes the need for student participation in the process of planning a curriculum or program. Widespread faculty participation is also necessary.

> The instructional program actually operates in terms of the learning experiences which the students have. Unless the objectives are clearly understood by each teacher, unless he is familiar with the kinds of learning experiences that can be used to attain these objectives, and unless he is able to guide the activities of students so that they will get these experiences, the educational program will not be an effective instrument for promoting the aims of the school. Hence, every teacher needs to participate in curriculum planning at least to the extent of gaining an adequate understanding of these ends and means.[81]

Business, industry, and labor likewise need to participate in career education. According to Gene Hensley and Mark Schulman, leaders in business, industry, and others outside of education are interested in career education for many of the same reasons given by educators. In particular, they cite such problems as the high dropout rate, the imbalance between students enrolled in college-preparatory programs as opposed to those enrolled in vocational-educational programs, and the relatively small number of students (23 percent of secondary school students) who actually graduate from college. [82]

Hensley and Schulman note that where significant partnerships between education and business have developed, there is a tendency for these relationships to grow and expand rather rapidly. Career education becomes a team effort once the representatives of business, industry, and education find that cooperative efforts are mutually beneficial. It is true that many business and industrial leaders have limited experience, if any, with career education, but such is also the case in many areas of education. "The important point is that there are many cases of major involvement of business and industry in career education programs, and many examples of cooperative efforts that have gone considerably beyond a participatory relationship. "[83]

Implementing the career-education concept is a major possible direction in which U.S. higher education may need to change. Most of today's students regard education as preparation for work. Kenneth B. Hoyt consequently recommends a number of curricular changes consistent with the concept of career education.

1. A shift toward recognizing and providing opportunities for some combination of a liberal-arts education and specific vocational skill training for all students;

2. An encouragement of the liberal-arts teaching faculty to recognize consciously and to emphasize the contributions of a liberal-arts education to achieving the goal of education as preparation for work;

3. A campuswide emphasis on providing career development opportunities for all students, one involving both the teaching faculty and student-personnel workers;

4. An encouragement of quality education through a competency-oriented, performance-based approach to evaluating instruction;

5. A campuswide emphasis on the broad, generic goals of higher education, which extend beyond the mere goal of education

as preparation for work—in the absence of such a change, any career-education effort will inevitably be faced with the proverbial "pendulum" problem, having a predictably limited life;

    6. An expansion of the ways in which higher education serves older adults as well as recent high school graduates.[84]

The last of these six recommendations is especially significant in view of the increasing number of adults that have been returning to school for one reason or another. Career problems for middle-aged adults are somewhat different from those faced by younger job seekers. Unemployment looms as a major economic threat for those middle-aged workers who are laid off. Once laid off, older workers find it quite difficult to secure suitable reemployment. Middle-aged workers may encounter psychological problems, especially where there has developed a discrepancy between achievement and aspiration. Older workers must, in many instances, reevaluate their life goals.

Problems may pile up for the older worker in a way that creates a vicious circle. An older worker may, for example, have problems making ends meet, which in turn may influence achievement motivation and morale, eventually leading to a layoff. Once laid off, the older worker's negative attitude may interfere in finding suitable reemployment.

In most problems affecting the middle-aged or older worker, it is evident that various economic, physical, and social psychological factors may be involved. The three solutions commonly offered (second careers, job redesign, and retraining) may affect each factor of the problem separately, in an additive manner, or in a complex interactive way. Further research is needed to determine the best predictors of job success for middle-aged or older workers, as well as the best method of training and job placement.

The cause of career education might be furthered if career education were integrated into teacher preparation. According to Brenda B. Even, there has been little emphasis on career education at the preservice level. She feels it essential that career education be made a part of existing teacher-preparation programs. For this purpose, she offers a model involving individual core courses, with emphasis on objectives, suggested activities, evaluation, and resources.[85]

According to Even, if a university or college is seeking to integrate career education into its existing teacher-preparation programs, it should establish a career information center for this purpose. On-campus activities would include the demonstration, production, and/or collection of career-education materials. Such "hands-on" experiences are vital to the development of teacher expertise and require field participation. There are four developmental stages for such a center:

1. The AWARENESS or perception stage in which the Center is used as a personal resource.
2. The ORIENTATION or investigation stage during which the Center serves a World of Work Resource.
3. The EXPLORATION or in-depth examination stage where the Center becomes a curriculum resource.
4. The PREPARATION or readiness stage in which the Center is designated as a student teaching and vocational resource. [86]

Career-development programs may confront obstacles that go far beyond expertise in project development. For example, despite the emergence of new, positive work values, the prospect of alienation from the work environment looms large in modern society. Karl Marx defined alienation as the separation of the worker from the so-called means of production, something that presumably is most indigenous to industrialized, capitalistic society. Emile Durkheim used the term anomia to indicate a similar idea. Anomia involves a sense of disorientation, anxiety, and isolation in the individual. It presumably evolves from anomie, a condition of society where normative standards of conduct and belief are weak.

Modern definitions of alienation are more general and comprehensive than these earlier descriptions. Alienation involves noninvolvement, an inability to develop firm commitments on the part of the individual, a social/psychological separation in which the worker literally turns away from a job. There are feelings of separateness and apartness, resulting in turbulence and distrust. The discrepancy between the individual's standards and social values may lead to conditions or feelings of powerlessness, meaninglessness, normlessness, cultural estrangement, self-estrangement, and social isolation.

Alienation has been attributed to a variety of causes, such as lack of stimulus, narrow work roles and overdivision of labor, personality and social dysfunctions, too much emphasis on rules, lack of information, authoritarianism in supervision, economic deprivation, lack of freedom, isolation from fellow workers, emphasis on quantity rather than quality, limited learning opportunities, and the rise of modern technology and the industrial society. Automation may reduce job meaning by eliminating direct work participation and variety. Where senior employees do not get promoted, there is a feeling of alienation.

Means of reducing alienation have been variously suggested. In some situations, authority lines have been simplified and clarified, communication channels increased, and the chains of command shortened for purposes of reducing alienation. Getting to know and take an interest in employees, more job responsibility, and other benefits have been successfully tried by some corporations. Suggested solutions include full employment, housing programs, expansion of subsidy programs, national health insurance, higher educational opportunities, retirement provisions, and pension plans geared to the needs of the blue-collar worker. Other proposed solutions include equalization of job amenities, freedom to rearrange tasks, union improvement and power, training sessions and effective education, change in job responsibilities to suit the needs of the employee, and responsiveness to individuals and groups on the part of the institution. Further suggestions include management therapy programs, freedom of the operator to determine pace and sequence, greater worker control over the development and governance of their work groups, pay on a group basis, and group rewards.

BUSINESS EDUCATION PROGRAMS

There is no ready agreement concerning what should be taught at some particular level of business education. Lee and Eileen Gentry, for example, listed the following 12 major concept areas for business ownership and management courses at the junior college level: economic systems, economic decision making, organizational structure, management principles, marketing factors, accounting, legal obligations, financial structure, risk taking and insurance, taxes, data processing, and social responsibility. The specific courses covering these major concept areas may vary from institution to institution or from program to program, depending on an individual institution's objectives.[87]

In 1964, B. G. Rainey conducted an in-depth analysis of the business programs of eight senior colleges and 15 junior colleges in Oklahoma. The six most important findings of the study were the following:

1. Extreme variations were observed in lower-division requirements at the senior institutions, both in business and in general education.

2. A considerable number of "nontransferable averages" was noted for students moving from the junior college to the senior college.

3. No clear distinction was made between "terminal" courses and "transfer" courses. In fact, not one of the 15 junior colleges studied labeled even a single business subject as "terminal."

4. Grade level, credits, titles, numbers, and course descriptions of business subjects varied significantly.

5. The average transfer business student took 18 semester hours of business subjects while at the junior college. Many of the courses taken most frequently were not transferable to the senior college (business law, marketing, business mathematics, and salesmanship, for instance).

6. The average junior college transfer student had to extend his senior college program 1.2 semesters as a result of such nontransferability.

Rainey's conclusions and recommendations follow:

1. Course numbering, credit, grade level, and course descriptions must be made more uniform within and between junior and senior colleges.

2. Subjects taken out of sequence cause much of the difficulty encountered by transfer students.

3. Senior colleges must standardize requirements.

4. Better control must be exercised over junior college business offerings (especially in upper-division and elective work in which there is no senior college counterpart). [88]

Kitty Locker noted that a major charge leveled against business communication courses is that they are not "respectable" and lack inherent academic substance and rigor. Locker concedes the absence of a clearly defined sense of what it is that must be done in business communication courses. She recommends that such courses place more emphasis on communications, rhetoric, linguistics, business administration, and psychology. Also recommended are expanded contacts by teachers of such courses with business and government. [89]

George Steiner enumerated a number of the new forces militating in favor of curriculum change in schools of business management. First, the relationships between business and the total environment are changing. New codes of ethics and corporate structures are taking root while social audits are becoming accepted. Business corruption and environmental pollution cause corporations to score poorly in public opinion polls. Business schools, says Steiner, must confront such social issues head-on. [90]

Second, business schools must address themselves on a larger scale to the not-for-profit sector. Steiner recommends new courses of study introduced primarily for students intending to enter the not-for-profit sector, although there is no need for programs concerned exclusively with this sector.

Third, schools must train problem finders as well as problem solvers. The student most brilliantly prepared in quantitative analysis must first recognize crucial problems before he can attempt solving them.

Fourth, students must be taught how to deal with "broad, messy, unstructured problems" which simply do not lend themselves to routine solution with the usual academic tools. Unfortunately, neither may they lend themselves to any other kind of academic treatment.

Fifth, curricula ought to be a blend of different approaches to management theory and practice, including the operational, organizational, behavioral, and quantitative approaches.

Sixth, strategy needs to be emphasized more strongly determining the fundamental purposes, directions, philosophy, and missions of an organization; the master policies guiding actions designed to achieve these aims; and the significant decisions concerning the acquisition, allocation, and disposition of resources to achieve organizational ends. [91]

Seventh, more courses concerning small business entrepreneurship are needed to satisfy the increasing demand for them.

In pursuit of the last-named objective, Arlo D. Stevick developed an educational and counseling system to educate and assist the small business entrepreneur on a continuing basis for a period of three years. The project was designed to operate a small business management program for 11 months a year over a two-year period. Enrollment in the program for the first year was limited to 20 businesses in the Lake Region area within a 60-mile radius of Devils Lake, North Dakota; an additional 20 businesses were enrolled for the second year. The instructional program was divided into four kinds of activities: classroom instruction including business analysis, small-group instruction, individual instruction, and business-technology instruction.[92]

Businesses are increasingly forming separate departments responsible for corporate communication (internal and external, with employees and with the public), requiring individuals with a strong background in, and an understanding of, the behavioral complexities of information flow, persuasion, attitude change, and opinion leadership. Herbert W. Hildebrandt and others recommended a minimum of 24 semester hours in business communication for the Master of Business Administration (MBA) program.[93] However, in common with so much of the literature reviewed in this chapter, they recognize that no single program is appropriate for all institutions.

With the proliferation of the consumer movement in the United States, many businesses have established consumer relations departments. Max O. McKitrick recommends a new curriculum for collegiate schools of business to meet this new situation.[94] Some authorities even recommend modeling English instruction on the basis of job-market needs,[95] modeling communication and language instruction after the needs of business and the job market to a greater extent than heretofore. Paul Kim stressed the need to develop more effectively the personal economic understanding of students through a relevant curriculum that includes an emphasis on consumerism.[96]

Alphonzo Sutherland points out the necessity for a fuller commitment to an improved blend of traditional methods and selected new techniques of individualized instruction.[97] Although there is no indication that business programs must change their basic structure, research indicates that changes are being made in curriculum, the use of multimedia and technology for mass instruction, the individualization of instruction, the use of newer methods and techniques, and providing new materials for use in teaching.

In a four-year college school of business, the department head can play a vital role in developing a sound business program. According to Larry Fiber, those major responsibilities include the areas of curriculum development, staffing, budgeting, scheduling, guidance, placement, innovation and experimentation, publication, professional improvement, and public relations.[98]

Lorraine A. Krajewski emphasizes the role of business educators as futurists. For instance, an office practice class could study the changing nature of office work, create future want ads, and role-play job interviews. A distributive education class could invent future goods and services, creating advertisements for them. An accounting class could be introduced to computerized accounting through the medium of a field trip to a local computerized business. "A gradual and balanced use of future oriented materials and activities will enable our students to better confront, cope with, and create their future."[99]

NOTES

1. Bulletin of Bryant College, Smithfield, R.I. (1980), p. 58.

2. Norman C. Harris and John F. Grede, Career Education in Colleges (San Francisco: Jossey-Bass, 1977), p. 2.

3. Robert A. Gordon and James E. Howell, Higher Education for Business (New York: Columbia University Press, 1959), p. 1.

4. Frank C. Pierson et al., The Education of American Businessmen: A Study of University College Programs in Business Administration (New York: McGraw-Hill, 1959), p. 3.

5. John J. Clark and Blaise J. Opulente, The Impact of the Foundation Reports on Business Education (New York: St. John's University Press, 1963), p. 21.

6. Frank K. Flaumenhaft, "The Undergraduate Curriculum in Business Education," Collegiate News and Views 31 (Fall 1977): 15-17.

7. Frank Watson, An Analysis of the Business Curriculum (Cincinnati, Ohio: South-Western, 1966), p. 1.

8. Flaumenhaft, "Undergraduate Curriculum," pp. 15-17.

9. Herman Berliner, "Real Economic Benefits of Higher Education," Personnel Journal, February 1971, p. 125.

10. Roger Gregoire, The University Teaching of Social Sciences: Business Management (Paris: United Nations Educational, Scientific, and Cultural Organization, 1966), p. 15.

11. Andrew C. Wallace, "Education in Business Administration: Image and Implication," Collegiate News and Views 25 (Spring 1972): 4.

12. D. Berry, "Management Education in American Schools," Economist, August 12, 1977, pp. 68-70.

13. Flaumenhaft, "Undergraduate Curriculum," p. 17.

14. William E. Cayley and Thomas W. Harold, "Which Way in a Program Change, Content or Method? One Response," Collegiate News and Views 33 (Winter 1979-80): 13.

15. T. R. Brannen, "Stages and Problems of Curriculum Transition," AACSB Bulletin 5 (October 1968): 1-21.

16. Cayley and Harold, "Which Way," p. 14.

17. Don L. James and Ronald L. Decker, "Does Business Student Preparation Satisfy Personnel Officers?" Collegiate News and Views 27 (Spring 1974): 26-29.

18. Cayley and Harold, "Which Way," p. 17.

19. Robert Cooper, "Alienation from Work," New Society 30 (January 1969): 161-63.

20. Worker Alienation (Scarsdale, N.Y.: Work in America Institute, n.d.), p. 3.

21. Ibid.

22. Robert Graham and Milton Valentine, "Alienation through Isolation," Personnel Administration 32 (March/April 1969): 16-20.

23. John Sweetland, Occupational Stress and Productivity (Scarsdale, N.Y.: Work in America Institute, n.d.), p. 8.

24. Stanley Nollen, New Patterns of Work (Scarsdale, N.Y.: Work in America Institute, n.d.), p. 12.

25. Robert P. Clark, "Business Enterprises Education Program: A Course for Supervisors," New Outlook, March 1974, pp. 128-31.

26. Ridley J. Gros, "The Communications Package in the Business Curriculum: Why?" ABCA Bulletin 39 (December 1976): 5-8.

27. J. Richard Hackman and Mary Dean Lee, Redesigning Work: A Strategy for Change (Scarsdale, N.Y.: Work in America Institute, n.d.), p. 35.

28. Edgar H. Schein, "Changing Role of the Personnel Manager" (Keynote address at the CUPA Eastern Regional Convention, Newton, Massachusetts, April 1975), p. 3.

29. John A. Beckett, Management Dynamics: The New Synthesis (New York: McGraw-Hill, 1971), p. 137.

30. Ibid., p. 199.

31. Marie DiVincenti, Administering Nursing Service (Boston: Little, Brown, 1975), p. 75.

32. Douglas C. Basil, Managerial Skills for Executive Action (New York: American Management Association, 1970), p. 38.

33. Chris Argyris, Management and Organizational Development (New York: McGraw-Hill, 1971), p. ix.

34. Ibid., p. x.

35. Ibid., p. 22.

36. Paul Mali, Managing by Objectives (New York: Wiley-Interscience, 1972), p. 2.

37. Frank E. Fischer and Lydia Strong, "Introduction: 'X Factor' in the Management Job," in Effective Communication on the Job, ed. Elizabeth Marting, Robert E. Finley, and Ann Ward (New York: American Management Association, 1963), p. 15.

38. William F. Keefe, Listen, Management: Creative Listening for Better Managing (New York: McGraw-Hill, 1971), p. 13.

39. Guy B. Ford, Building a Winning Employee Team (New York: American Management Association, 1964), p. 10.

40. Ibid., p. 17.

41. Thomas F. Stroh, Managing the New Generation in Business (New York: McGraw-Hill, 1971), p. 22.

42. Peter F. Drucker, Management (New York: Harper and Row, 1974), p. x.

43. Jerome M. Rosow, "Quality of Work Life Issues for the 1980s," Training and Development Journal, March 1981, p. 47.

44. B. Bertha Wakin, "Competency-Based Teacher Education: Boon or Bane in Business Education Programs?" Journal of Business Education 53 (January 1978): 170-71.

45. John E. Graham, "Competency-Based Accounting Instruction," Journal of Business Education, January 1977, p. 184.

46. Ibid., p. 186.

47. Joseph P. Giusti and George R. Lovette, "The Business School in Higher Education," Journal of Business Education, January 1971, p. 42.

48. David T. Borland, "Organizational Action Process" (Address to the Annual Convention of the American College Personnel Association, Atlanta, Georgia, March 5-8, 1975), p. 7.

49. Ibid., p. 4.

50. Ibid.

51. Laurence A. Brown, Employment of an Open Learning Course with Traditional and Nontraditional Learners (Washington, D.C.: National Institute of Education, 1976), p. 15.

52. Ibid., p. 24.

53. Joel Podell, Abraham Axelrod, Jonas Falik, and Dennis Green, "The Introductory College Business Course: A New Dimension," Journal of Business Education, May 1977, p. 352.

54. Ibid., p. 353.

55. Marguerite E. Donovan, "Business, Liberal Arts, and the Transfer Student," Journal of Business Education, January 1976, pp. 87-88.

56. John M. Kuhlman, "The Impact of Quantitative Analysis in the College of Business," Collegiate News and Views 15 (October 1961): 7-10.

57. Roger L. Burford and Donald R. Williams, "Quantitative Methods in the Undergraduate Curricula of AACSB Member Institutions," Decision Sciences 3 (January 1972): 111-27.

58. James C. Van Pelt and Edwin C. Spencer, "The Quantitative Curricula of AACSB Accredited Undergraduate Business Schools," AACSB Bulletin, Spring 1977, pp. 11-16.

59. Daryl Nord and Tom Seymour, "Yes! The Business Department Teaches Data Processing," Balance Sheet, March 1978, p. 282.

60. National Commission for Cooperative Education, Undergraduate Programs of Cooperative Education (Boston: Northeastern University, 1977), p. 21.

61. Joe Thomas, "Operating Characteristics of Cooperative Education Programs in Business Schools," Journal of Cooperative Education 16 (1979): 31.

62. Christopher G. L. Pratt, "Survey of Attitudes toward Cooperative Education," Journal of Cooperative Education 16 (1979): 36-37.

63. Ibid.

64. Gerard E. Nistal, "Is Higher Education Responsive to the Needs of the Real World of Business?" Collegiate News and Views 33 (Winter 1979-80): 10.

65. Richard Dieffenderfer, Lee Kopp, and Orest Cap, Business-Industry-Labor Linkages: A Handbook for Improving Personnel Development Programs (Columbus: Ohio State University, 1977), p. 17.

66. Clifford L. Rall and Frank E. O'Brien, Methods and Procedures for Job Identification and Placement Based upon Industrial Needs (Washington, D.C.: Office of Education, 1977), p. ii.

67. Benton E. Miles, "Developing Distributive Education Programs," in Curriculum Development in Education for Business, ed. James W. Crews and Z. S. Dickerson, Jr. (Reston, Va.: National Business Education Association, 1977), p. 179.

68. Ibid., p. 191.

69. Clifton R. Wharton, "Career Education at the College Level," Today's Education, April-May 1976, p. 74.

70. Ibid.

71. Daniel Yankelovich, "The New Psychological Contracts at Work," Psychology Today 2 (May 1978): 47.

72. Ibid., p. 48.

73. Patricia A. Renwick and Edward E. Lawler, "What You Really Want from Your Job," Psychology Today 11 (May 1978): 118.

74. Roger E. Calhoun, "The New Work Ethic," Training and Development Journal, May 1980, p. 127.

75. Ibid., p. 130.

76. Phillip M. Hauser, "Education and Careers—Concordant or Discordant" (Address to the National Meeting of the College Placement Council, Washington, D.C., May 28, 1975), p. 2.

77. Lorraine S. Hansen, An Examination of the Definitions and Concepts of Career Education (Washington, D.C.: National Advisory Council for Career Education, 1977), p. 39.

78. Derek Bok, quoted in "Graduates: Ill Prepared for Business?" Worcester Gazette (Massachusetts), March 30, 1979, p. 2.

79. Claus Reschke, "Career Education at the College Level: A Modest Proposal" (Paper presented at the Annual Meeting of the American Association of Teachers of German, Philadelphia, August 1976), p. 1.

80. "What's New in Career Development," Career Development Bulletin 1 (Spring 1979): 1.

81. Ralph W. Tyler, Basic Principles of Curriculum and Instruction (Chicago: University of Chicago Press, 1949), p. 126.

82. Gene Hensley and Mark Schulman, Two Studies on the Role of Business and Industry and Labor Participation in Career Education (Washington, D.C.: National Advisory Council for Career Education, June 1977), p. 5.

83. Ibid.

84. Kenneth B. Hoyt, Considerations of Career Education in Postsecondary Education (Washington, D.C.: HEW Monographs on Career Education, 1978), pp. 7-8.

85. Brenda B. Even, Integrating Career Education into Teacher Preparation (Washington, D.C.: U.S. Government Printing Office, 1976), p. 24.

86. Ibid.

87. Lee Gentry and Eileen Gentry, "Business Management Concept Areas for Two-Year Postsecondary Institutions," Business Education Forum, April 1978, pp. 37-38.

88. B. G. Rainey, "Articulation in Collegiate Education for Business," Ph.D. dissertation, University of Oklahoma, 1964, p. 139.

89. Kitty Locker, "Making Business Communication Courses Academically Respectable," ABCA Bulletin, March 1979, pp. 6-10.

90. George Steiner, "Future Curricula in Schools of Management," AACSB Bulletin 13 (October 1976): 7.

91. Ibid., p. 9.

92. Arlo D. Stevick, Model for Small Business Management Program in North Dakota Post-Secondary Institutions (Bismarck: North Dakota State Board for Vocational Education, 1978), p. 19.

93. Herbert W. Hildebrandt et al., "Proposal for a Master of Business Administration in Business Communication," ABCA Bulletin, March 1977, pp. 3-7.

94. Max McKitrick, "Consumer Relations: A New Curriculum for Collegiate Schools of Business," Journal of Business Education, May 1977, pp. 350-52.

95. Lean B. Prewitt, "Research in Office Practice," Office Practice Program in Business Education (Somerville, Mass.: Eastern Business Teachers Association) 46 (1969): 33.

96. Paul Kim, "Personal Economic Understanding and College Business and Economics Courses," Delta Pi Epsilon Journal 19 (April 1977): 22-35.

97. Alphonzo Sutherland, "An Evaluation of Individualized Instruction for Evening/Part-Time Students of Business," Practicum presented to Nova University in partial fulfillment of the requirements for the Doctor of Education degree, Fort Lauderdale, Fla., May 1975, p. 3.

98. Larry Fiber, "The Role of the Department Chairman at Different Levels of Business Education," Business Education Forum, May 1972, pp. 37-39.

99. Lorraine A. Krajewski, "Business Educators as Futurists," Journal of Business Education, January 1977, p. 174.

3
METHODOLOGY

The empirical part of the study involved selecting a sample, distributing four questionnaires, collecting data, and analyzing data. The overall procedure is described below.

THE SAMPLE

The sample consisted of the following four groups:

1. Upper-division students (100 juniors and seniors) at Bryant College (Smithfield, Rhode Island) or at Worcester State College (Worcester, Massachusetts); and another 100 students at eight other colleges in Massachusetts (see map in Appendix A). Half of the sample members were selected randomly from lists of students in the various business departments. The remaining sample members were selected by members of the respective faculties.

2. The 50 faculty members currently teaching upper-division, business administration courses at the ten colleges.

3. Alumni, totaling 100, of the schools of business administration of Bryant College and Worcester State College. Their

names and addresses were obtained from the alumni offices of the two schools.

    4. Business organizations, also totaling 100, that have hired and supervised graduates of Bryant College, Worcester State College, Nichols College, Clark University, and Anna Maria College. Half of the business organizations were contacted by mail; the others were contacted personally by the researcher. Those contacted included personnel managers, supervisors, and managers.

THE FOUR INSTRUMENTS

    The four instruments (questionnaires) used in the empirical part of the study are reproduced, respectively, in Appendixes B, C, D, and E—one questionnaire for each of the four sample groups. The questionnaires collected data relating to the nine aspects of business administration programs enumerated in the statement-of-the-purpose section in Chapter 1 of this text.

    Responses to most of the questionnaire items were solicited on finite or closed-ended Likert-type scales. Three kinds of scales were used for these items. The first kind presented five choices, ranging from "agree strongly" (weighted with a value of 5) to "disagree strongly" (weighted with a value of 1). The second kind of scale offered three choices: "yes," "no," and "I don't know." The third kind of scale provided four choices, ranging from "extremely helpful" (weighted with a value of 4) to "I don't know" (weighted with a value of 1). Useful biographical and demographic data were, in addition, solicited by means of a few preliminary questions included at the beginning of each questionnaire.

    Some infinite or open-ended responses were also encouraged by the questionnaires. Respondents were asked to explain their reasons for their answers to some of the questions. Respondents were also asked to present their opinions concerning specific changes they would like to make in the business administration programs familiar to them.*

---

*Similar questionnaires and methodologies were used by Adames in his study of distributive education in the State of New Hampshire.

ANALYSIS OF DATA

The data were presented and analyzed in two ways. First, a sample profile was prepared based on a descriptive summary of each group's responses to each questionnaire item. The profile indicated how the sample as a whole responded to the various issues and questions. It also showed how each of the four individual groups responded.

Second, mean-sample responses to various questionnaire items were compared in order to determine the statistical significance, if any, of the difference observed. For this purpose, statistical t-tests were employed, seeking at least the .05 level of confidence.

The results of these analyses were then combined with the findings of the earlier literature review in order to construct a preferred set of guidelines for collegiate business administration programs.

4

PRESENTATION AND
ANALYSIS OF RESULTS

This chapter presents and analyzes the results of the empirical part of the study. Table 1 summarizes the data concerning the four sample sizes and the number of usable questionnaires obtained from each sample.

TABLE 1

Number of Usable Questionnaires Obtained
from Each of the Four Study Samples

Group	Sample Size	Usable Questionnaires Obtained	Percent Obtained
Students	200	65	33
Faculty	50	36	72
Alumni	100	51	51
Business managers	100	54	54

GROUP CHARACTERISTICS

Section A of each questionnaire asked the respondents to provide demographic and other pertinent information about themselves.

Students

Of the students questioned, 62 percent were male, 38 percent female. Of the 65 students, 17 percent had participated in a business administration program for one year, 34 percent for two years, 29 percent for three years, and 20 percent for four years. Accordingly, there was a reasonably balanced overall representation with respect to sex and years of experience in the business administration program.

Most of the students, after completing the business administration program, planned either to seek full-time employment related to the area of their study (45 percent), to work full-time in order to attend graduate school part-time (29 percent), or to begin full-time graduate study (14 percent); 12 percent were undecided about their future plans. Seven out of every eight, therefore, planned definitely to continue in activities connected with business.

In giving reasons for choosing a specific business administration program, most respondents stated that there were many good jobs related to that field of study (51 percent) or that it was their desire to develop specific skills currently in demand (32 percent). The rest of the respondents (24 percent) stated that the college offered no other programs of interest, the business administration program was recommended by other individuals, they were not sure why they had made their choice, and/or gave some miscellaneous reasons. Accordingly, most students were career-oriented in their choice of program.

Faculty Members

Of the faculty members questioned, 89 percent were male, 11 percent female. Of the 36 faculty members, only 17 percent had less than three years of teaching experience; 33 percent had between three and six years of experience; and 50 percent had more than six years of experience. The faculty members were, therefore, predominantly male and with at least a good degree of experience.

A majority of the faculty members had either worked in a business-administration-related occupation (69 percent) or had taught college business administration courses somewhere else (25 percent) before becoming business administration faculty members at their current affiliation.

Alumni

Of the alumni questioned, 61 percent were male, 39 percent female. Of the 100 alumni, 37 percent had graduated two to three years ago; 41 percent had graduated four to five years ago; and only 1 percent had graduated six or more years ago. Accordingly, most of the alumni were recent graduates.

As regarded employment classification, 31 percent of the alumni were currently in manufacturing; 16 percent were in retail establishments; and 12 percent were in travel and/or lodging. The remaining 41 percent were in other occupations including sales representation, service industry, insurance sales, construction, education (including the university level), banking, food services, public utility, government agency, hospital administration, wholesaling, and nonprofit organizations. Thus, the graduates were in many different lines of work.

As to how they secured their present employment, some 38 percent said that they had answered an advertisement in a local newspaper. Others listed employment agencies (18 percent) and referral by another employee (18 percent). Only 6 percent were selected in on-campus college recruiting. Another 6 percent answered an advertisement in a professional or trade journal, while 16 percent gave other explanations, such as going into the family business. It is, consequently, evident that the business organizations did not actively seek and hire business majors; the business graduate had to go out and seek a job on his own.

Business Managers

Of the 54 business managers responding, 60 percent stated that their firms employed 500 or more persons. Another 28 percent employed fewer than 100 persons; 12 percent, between 100 and 500 persons. The firms in the sample were, therefore, a fairly good cross section of large and small business organizations.

Of the responding firms, 72 percent had graduates of business administration programs working for them for six or more years. Among the remaining 28 percent, some 15 percent had such employees working for them between four and five years; 13 percent for three or fewer years. This breakdown indicated a reasonably good familiarity with the products of schools of business administration.

A majority of the firms (54 percent) were engaged in manufacturing, 11 percent were retail establishments, and 6 percent were travel and/or lodging establishments; 29 percent of the firms were other kinds of establishments, including firms in banking, insurance, service, accounting, wholesaling, and the military.

The business managers listed a number of ways in which they hired business administration graduates: employment agencies (43 percent), advertisements in professional or trade journals (19 percent), advertisements in local newspapers (39 percent), on-campus college recruiting (62 percent), and employee referrals (33 percent); 9 percent of the sample reported other means such as personal recruitment and contact through internship programs. These data correspond reasonably well with those obtained from the alumni regarding how they secured positions.

THE SAMPLE PROFILE

Analysis of Table 2

The sample profile was established chiefly on the basis of the four mean-group responses to the items in Section B of the questionnaires. Responses to these items were made on a scale ranging from 1 (disagree strongly) to 5 (agree strongly). Table 2 lists the four mean-group responses to the 13 items in Part I of Section B inquiring into the purpose of business administration programs.

Item 1: Significantly more so than the students (3.4) or the faculty members (3.4), the alumni (3.8) believed that business administration programs should prepare students for jobs, although not necessarily in business administration ($p < .05$).* The students,

---

*Statistical t-tests were used to determine whether or not two means were significantly different. The notation "$p < .05$"

faculty members, and business managers (3.6) were only moderately in agreement with this item.

Item 2: All four groups tended to agree with the idea that business administration programs should be geared toward helping students define personal goals. However, the student group (3.8) was significantly less ($p < .01$) in favor of this purpose than were either faculty members (4.3) or alumni (4.4).

Item 3: The students (4.1) and alumni (4.3) were significantly more in favor of business administration programs that prepare students in areas related directly to their fields of study ($p < .01$). The faculty members' mean of 3.7 and business managers' mean of 3.6 indicated only mild agreement with this purpose. Faculty members and business managers attributed significantly less urgency to academic programs preparing students to specialize immediately than did students and alumni. The reasons for this difference of opinion will be noted later in the discussion of questionnaire Section D; some business managers asserted that actual training for a job only takes place on the job itself.

Item 4: The four group means ranged from 4.1 to 4.4, indicating that the four groups were equally strongly in favor of helping students explore career opportunities related to their fields of study.

Item 5: The four group means ranged from 4.1 to 4.4, indicating that all four groups were equally strongly in favor of preparing students for better positions than might otherwise be available to them.

Item 6: The students (3.7), faculty members (3.6), and business managers (3.6) were only mildly in favor of designing business administration programs to assist students in finding full-time positions. However, the alumni's mean score of 4.2 was significantly more in agreement with this purpose ($p < .01$). It seems logical that alumni holding degrees in business administration would be greatly concerned with obtaining full-time positions.

Item 7: Faculty (4.4) and alumni (4.5) were significantly more concerned than were students (4.0) and business managers 4.1) that business administration programs should give students a better understanding of what careers they want to pursue. However, all four groups were in decidedly strong agreement with this purpose.

---

states that two means are significantly different at the .05 level of confidence.

TABLE 2

Mean Responses of Students, Faculty, Alumni, and Managers to Items Relating
to the Purpose of Business Administration Programs

| Item | Mean Group Scores | | | |
	Students	Faculty Members	Alumni	Business Managers
The purpose of business administration programs should be:				
1. To prepare students for jobs, but not necessarily in business administration	3.4	3.4	3.8	3.6
2. To help students define personal goals	3.8	4.3	4.4	4.1
3. To prepare students for positions related directly to their fields of study	4.1	3.7	4.3	3.6
4. To help students explore career opportunities related to their fields of study	4.4	4.3	4.4	4.1
5. To prepare students for better positions than might otherwise be available to them	4.2	4.2	4.4	4.1

6. To assist students in finding full-time positions	3.7	3.6	4.2	3.6
7. To give students a better understanding of what careers they wish to pursue	4.0	4.4	4.5	4.1
8. To help students develop both basic and advanced skills in the chosen area of study	4.8	4.7	4.6	4.2
9. To help students develop the proper attitudes and perspectives needed to do well in positions related to their chosen fields	4.4	4.4	4.6	4.6
10. To teach the communication skills involved in getting along with superiors, subordinates, and colleagues	4.5	4.3	4.5	4.6
11. To strengthen students' vocational self-confidence	4.3	4.4	4.3	4.3
12. To assist students in discovering their own identity	3.6	3.9	3.8	4.0
13. To help students develop leadership potential	4.3	3.9	4.4	4.1

Item 8: All four groups were noticeably in favor of business administration programs that help students explore career opportunities related to their fields of study. The mean scores of students (4.8), faculty members (4.7), and alumni (4.6) were significantly higher (p < .01) than that of business managers (4.2).

Item 9: All four groups were strongly in favor of using business administration programs to help students develop both the attitudes and the perspectives necessary to do well in positions related to their chosen fields. Mean scores ranged from 4.4 to 4.6 and were not significantly different from each other.

Item 10: All four groups were strongly in favor of teaching communication skills involved in getting along with superiors, subordinates, and colleagues. The scores ranged from 4.3 to 4.6 and were not significantly different from each other.

Item 11: All four groups were strongly in favor of programs strengthening students' self-confidence. The scores ranged from 4.3 to 4.4 and were not significantly different from each other.

Item 12: On the whole, all of the four groups were fairly strong in the belief that programs should assist students in discovering their self-identities. The business managers' mean score of 4.0 was significantly higher than was the students' mean score of 3.6. Business managers are evidently more often in direct contact with the practical problem of employees who are not certain about what they really wish to do, therefore probably displaying the greatest concern about the problem.

Item 13: All four groups were in strong agreement that business administration programs should help students develop leadership potential. The faculty members' mean score of 3.9 was significantly lower (p < .05) than was the students' mean score of 4.3 or the alumni's mean score of 4.4. Faculty members and business managers were presumably less concerned with developing leadership potential than were students and alumni, possibly because the former two groups were afraid of having their own leadership too severely challenged.

Analysis of Table 3

Part II of Section B investigated business-administration-program determinants. Table 3 shows how the four groups responded to the three items in this part of the questionnaire.

TABLE 3

Mean Responses of Students, Faculty Members, and Business Managers to Items
concerning Business-Administration-Program Determinants

| | Mean Group Scores | | | |
Item	Students	Faculty Members	Alumni	Business Managers
1. The business administration faculty is in a good position to help determine what courses should be taught in business administration programs	3.7	4.0	3.9	3.6
2. The business community is in a good position to help determine what courses should be taught in business administration programs	3.8	4.0	4.0	4.1
3. The students enrolled in business administration programs are in a good position to help determine what courses should be taught in business administration programs	3.2	3.8	3.5	2.6

Item 1: The faculty members (4. 0) and the alumni (3. 9) agreed that the business administration faculty is in a good position to help determine what courses should be taught in business administration programs. The students (3. 7) and business managers (3. 6) were slightly less strongly in favor of this item, but not significantly so.

Item 2: All four groups were strong in their belief that the business community is in a good position to help determine what courses should be taught in business administration programs. The mean scores ranged from 3. 8 to 4. 1 and were not significantly different from each other. The mean of the four scores for item 2 is higher than the mean of the four scores for item 1, indicating that the four groups as a whole placed more emphasis on the business community than on faculties as a source of authority or information in determining the courses making up business administration programs. As might have been expected, the 4. 1 mean score of business managers on item 2 was significantly higher than was the 3. 6 mean score of business managers on item 1 (p $<$. 05). In effect, business managers regarded themselves as more qualified than faculties in determining the content of business administration programs.

Item 3: Significant differences between groups surfaced on this item. The business managers' mean score of 2. 6 indicated disagreement with the idea that students in business administration programs are in a good position to help determine what courses should be included in business administration programs. This mean score was significantly lower than the students' mean score of 3. 2 (p $<$. 01). The students' mean score of 3. 2 was, in turn, significantly lower than was the faculty members' mean score of 3. 8 (p $<$. 01). The faculty members and alumni (3. 5) were more or less in agreement, although not very strongly, that students should constitute a major input in determining program content. There was, accordingly, some disagreement on the question with students and business managers not particularly favoring student input, while faculty members and alumni were much more in favor of such input.

Analysis of Table 4

Part III of Section B concerned the selection criteria used in admitting students to business administration programs. Table 4 shows how the four groups responded to the three items in this part of the questionnaire.

TABLE 4

Mean Responses of Students, Faculty Members, Alumni, and Business Managers
to Items concerning Admission Criteria

Item	Mean Group Scores			
	Students	Faculty Members	Alumni	Business Managers
1. The admission of students into business administration programs should be determined by previous school grade point averages; recommendations from faculty members, counselors, and school administrators; entrance examinations; and/or other personal documentation	3.4	4.0	4.1	3.7
2. The admission of students into business administration programs should primarily be the responsibility of the business administration faculty	3.3	3.0	3.2	3.0
3. The admission of students into business administration programs should be determined by the students, who know whether they are suited for such programs	2.8	2.5	3.4	3.0

Item 1: Faculty members (4.0) and alumni (4.1) were in definite agreement with the idea that students should be selected on the basis of grade point averages, faculty recommendations, counselors' and school administrators' opinions, entrance examinations, and/or other personal documentation. The students (3.4) were significantly less in favor of this method ($p < .01$). The business managers (3.7) were between the other groups.

Item 2: None of the four groups particularly favored selecting students on the basis of business administration faculty judgment alone. The mean scores ranged from 3.0 to 3.3, with no significant differences between any two of them.

Item 3: None of the groups were particularly in favor of permitting students themselves to decide their qualifications for admission. The faculty members' mean score of 2.5 was significantly lower than was the alumni's mean of 3.4 ($p < .01$), with the student mean being 2.8 and that of business managers 3.0. On the whole, the scores seemed to indicate a neutral or uncertain response rather than definite opposition or a favorable stance.

Analysis of Table 5

Part IV of Section B concerned the internship-cooperative experience. Table 5 shows how the four groups responded to the two items in this part of the questionnaire.

Item 1: Students (4.4) and alumni (4.5) were particularly in favor of internship-cooperative programs within a business administration curriculum, as were business managers (4.1). The faculty members (3.8) were fairly strongly in favor of them, but significantly less so than either students or alumni ($p < .01$). It may be concluded that faculty members are significantly behind the other groups in advocating internship-cooperative curricula.

Item 2: The faculty members (3.3) were significantly ($p < .01$) less convinced than were all other groups that the internship-cooperative experience is essential in meeting the objectives of the business administration program. The business managers' mean score of 4.3, the students' mean score of 4.0, and the alumni's mean score of 4.5 all reflected a much stronger belief that such an experience is essential to business administration programs. There was, accordingly, a distinct division of opinion between faculty members and students, alumni, and business managers; the latter three groups were far more strongly convinced than were the

TABLE 5

Mean Responses of Students, Faculty Members, Alumni, and Business Managers
to Items concerning Internship–Cooperative Experiences

| Item | Mean Group Scores | | | |
	Students	Faculty Members	Alumni	Business Managers
1. The business internship–cooperative program within a business administration curriculum ought to be an integral part of a student's learning experience	4.4	3.8	4.5	4.1
2. The business internship–cooperative jobs that students hold while enrolled in business administration programs are essential to meeting the objectives of the program	4.0	3.3	4.5	4.3

faculty members that internship-cooperative jobs are essential in meeting the objectives of a business administration program.

Analysis of Table 6

Part V of Section B of the questionnaire concerned the role of the business administration faculty. Table 6 shows how the four groups responded to the three items in this unit of the question-naire.

Item 1: The students' mean score of 3.8 was significantly higher ($p < .05$) than were the corresponding means of faculty mem-bers (3.2), alumni (3.3), and business managers (3.1), as con-cerned faculty members providing vocational career counseling for students. Such a difference is logical, since faculty members, alumni, and business managers are in a better position than stu-dents to know that job training is normally received on the job, and that a precise science for determining the most suitable vocation one ought to follow does not exist.

Item 2: Students (4.1), alumni (4.1), and business managers (4.0) supported using the faculty to counsel and advise students in selecting courses fairly strongly. However, the faculty mem-bers' mean score of 3.4 was significantly lower ($p < .01$) than were the other three means, indicating that faculty members do not particularly favor such a role. Direct experience in this area may, perhaps, have made faculty members sensitive to the diffi-culties involved, and their responses may have reflected a realism born of experience.

Item 3: Here another polarity surfaced, one involving stu-dents and faculty members versus alumni and business managers; one concerning the idea of a close liaison between business ad-ministration faculties and the business community. The faculty members' mean score of 3.3 was significantly lower ($p < .01$) than were the alumni's mean of 4.6 and the business managers' mean of 4.1. The students' mean score of 3.7 was likewise significant-ly lower than was the alumni's mean of 4.6. Accordingly, the alumni and business managers were much more in favor of close contact between faculty and business community than were either students or faculty members.

TABLE 6

Mean Responses of Students, Faculty Members, Alumni, and Business Managers
to Items concerning the Role of the Business Administration Faculty

| | Mean Group Scores | | | |
Item	Students	Faculty Members	Alumni	Business Managers
1. A primary function of the business administration faculty ought to be to provide business administration students with vocational career counseling	3.8	3.2	3.3	3.1
2. A primary function of the business administration faculty ought to be to counsel and advise students in selecting courses	4.1	3.4	4.1	4.0
3. A primary function of the business administration faculty ought to be to work closely with the business community	3.7	3.3	4.6	4.1

Analysis of Table 7

Section C of the questionnaire probed the quality and relevance of business administration programs. Table 7 shows how the four study groups responded to two of the items in this part of the questionnaire.

Item 1: All four groups believed that business administration programs help students satisfy the requirements they must meet in order to be employed in responsible positions. The mean scores ranged from 3.0 to 3.2, well over the neutral score 2.5. Consequently, all four groups considered the programs fully relevant to the business world.

Item 2: On the whole, the four groups considered the business administration programs to be of good quality, with the mean group scores ranging from 2.7 to 3.1. Accordingly, the results for items 1 and 2 showed the four groups about equally convinced that business administration programs are both of good quality and professionally relevant.

Analysis of Table 8

Section C also included several questions relating only to faculty members, alumni, and business managers. Table 8 shows how these three groups responded to two questions concerning the adequacy of student preparation for jobs by business schools.

Item 1: All three groups believed that business administration programs are preparing students for jobs that would otherwise be unavailable to them. The mean scores ranged from 2.6 (business managers) to 2.8 (faculty members). The differences were statistically insignificant.

Item 2: All three groups believed that graduates of business administration programs are more adequately prepared for the business world than are students graduating from nonbusiness, academic degree programs, although with not as much conviction as they did in the case of item 1. The mean scores ranged from 2.4 to 2.7.

Another indication of the degree of support for these two items is provided by the percentage of each group answering "yes" to each item. In the case of item 1, 83 percent of the faculty members, 78 percent of the alumni, and 72 percent of the business

TABLE 7

Mean Responses of Students, Faculty Members, Alumni, and Business Managers
to Items Probing the Quality and Relevance
of Business Administration Programs

| | Mean Group Scores* | | | |
Item	Students	Faculty Members	Alumni	Business Managers
1. To what extent do you believe that business administration programs help students satisfy the requirements they must meet in order to be employed in responsible positions?	3.2	3.2	3.0	3.0
2. On the whole, how would you rate the quality of the business administration programs with which you have been involved?	2.9	3.1	2.8	2.7

*The middle or neutral score in this table is 2.5 instead of 3 because a four-point scale (ranging from 1 to 4) was used with these questions.

TABLE 8

Mean Responses of Faculty Members, Alumni, and Business Managers
to Items concerning the Adequacy of Job Preparation
in Schools of Business Administration

| Item | Mean Group Scores* | | |
	Faculty Members	Alumni	Business Managers
1. Do you feel that business administration programs are preparing students for jobs that would otherwise be unavailable to them?	2.8	2.7	2.6
2. In your opinion, are graduates of business administration programs more adequately prepared for the business world than are students graduating from nonbusiness academic degree programs?	2.4	2.7	2.5

*The middle or neutral mean score was 2.0. Respondents answered on the three-point scale "yes" (3), "I don't know" (2), and "no" (1).

managers answered "yes" to the statement. In the case of item 2, 58 percent of the faculty members, 80 percent of the alumni, and 65 percent of the business managers answered "yes" to the statement.

Question 31 of the questionnaire for business managers asked, Are you currently employing or have you previously employed graduates of business administration programs? The percentage of respondents replying that they had done so was 96, establishing that the business managers of the sample had had sufficient experience with the products of business administration programs to give their questionnaire responses.

Analysis of Table 9

Section C of the student questionnaire included a number of questions pertaining specifically to them. Table 9 lists the questions and how the students responded to them.

Item 1: A heavy majority (83 percent) of the students had enrolled in business administration programs because of career aspirations. Very few had chosen business administration programs for reasons other than career or work.

Item 2: A very heavy majority (88 percent) of the students expressed no regrets over having entered a business administration program. This majority stated that it would make the same choice again if faced with the same alternatives.

Item 3: Fewer than half of the students (42 percent) believed that their program was preparing them well for graduate study. Most of the others (47 percent) were uncertain, with only 11 percent stating that their program was not preparing them for graduate study.

Item 4: Only 42 percent of the students believed that their program had helped them choose a suitable career path. Of the others, 27 percent felt that it had not, and 31 percent were uncertain.

Item 5: A large majority (74 percent) of the students asserted that they would recommend their program to other students. Despite the uncertainty expressed in items 3 and 4, the students were nevertheless still positive about their own programs.

Item 6: Almost 80 percent of the students evaluated the quality of their business administration programs as either excellent (17 percent) or good (62 percent). This percentage is consistent

TABLE 9

Responses to Questionnaire Items concerning Students Only

Item	Percent of Students Choosing This Reason
1. For what reasons did you enroll in a business administration program?	
I have a career goal of working in some aspect of business administration	83
I want to acquire knowledge preparing me directly to enter the world of work	42
The program was recommended by my high school guidance counselor	5
Someone in my family majored in business administration and is now a successful business individual	9
Other reasons	5

	Responses of Students (in percent)		
	Yes	No	Unsure
2. If you had to choose a college program again, would you enroll in a business administration program?	88	5	7
3. Do you believe that your program is preparing you well for graduate studies?	42	11	47
4. Has your program helped you choose a suitable career path for yourself?	42	27	31
5. Would you recommend your program to other students?	74	8	18

	Response of Students (in percent)			
	Excellent	Good	Fair	Poor
6. How would you evaluate the overall quality of the business administration program in your college?	17	62	20	1

85

with the results of Table 7, showing that students rated their business administration programs as being of good quality and relevant.

As shown in Table 8, the faculty, alumni, and business managers responded to two items concerning adequacy of job preparation in schools of business administration. Each group was asked to give its reasons for any negative replies.

Some of the faculty members believed that schools of business administration—and other schools such as liberal arts schools—prepared their students about equally for the business world. Some respondents took issue with the wording better prepared in the questions. Typical comments included, "Better prepared for what?" "Better prepared compared to what?" and "Better prepared for all positions?" Some respondents complained that business graduates "cannot form sentences" and are unfamiliar with grammar and spelling. Others indicated that the graduates needed to be more familiar with the liberal arts. However, these comments came from a decided minority of those responding, with none of the faculty members believing that a degree in business administration failed to prepare students for jobs otherwise not available to them.

The comparatively few alumni who negatively assessed the adequacy of their school's preparation of students for jobs gave a number of reasons. Some commented that the market is saturated with business majors and that experience counts much more than does education in the business world. They asserted that what the schools teach is theory, whereas what is needed to obtain a job is practical, specialized knowledge. In this sense, it was evidently their opinion that the schools were not preparing students for jobs. Some respondents cited the need for exposing students more extensively to career opportunities, saying that "employers won't let an unproven college graduate move up." They also mentioned the need for more internship opportunities. They pointed out that many business school graduates had passed through programs that were general and theoretical, whereas the typical graduate actually enters a highly specific area such as sales. They also observed that business schools need to work more closely with the business community.

Although only a very small percentage of the business managers were negative concerning the adequacy of business school job preparation, a larger number of negative viewpoints was expressed by business managers than by faculty members or alumni. One manager contended that a degree was of secondary importance, that landing a job was more a matter of "being at the right place at the right time." Another manager believed that liberal-arts graduates can be trained for many business positions, while business school graduates are primarily useful in a few specialized positions. "We place emphasis on the individual rather than the degree." Liberal-arts skills can transfer to the requirements of the business situation and, according to one manager, much depends on individual goals, motivation, skills, and training.

RECOMMENDATIONS

In Section D of the questionnaire for each group, respondents were asked to recommend changes in college business administration programs to transform them into more valuable learning experiences.

Student Recommendations

One recommendation related to the quality of the teaching in business administration programs. Some students asserted that their instructors were teaching subjects for which they were not especially well prepared. A few mentioned "dull" teachers and the need for a greater variety of teachers "so that you don't have to meet them several times a day."

A closely related recommendation was that more of the professors come directly from, or be intimately connected with, the actual world of business. Other respondents recommended lectures from "real business people" and a more effective liaison between faculty members and the business community.

Mentioned more frequently than any other single factor was the need for internship-cooperative experiences. Specifically recommended were field work, courses in how to run a business, and more concern with the actual business world.

It was recommended that courses be less theoretical and more practical. Their emphasis should be on real business problems and case studies. One student pointed out that most students do not know how to obtain information and use it or how to conduct business research. Another student wanted "less lecture and more discussion." One recommendation for realistic orientation consisted of having a student search for a job.

Greater emphasis on basic communication skills was recommended, including more courses in public speaking, writing, personal development, and the liberal arts.

More and better counseling was recommended by a number of students. Some suggested more counseling with respect to what courses to take, with the counselors being more sincerely involved. Many students recommended more career counseling.

A number of recommendations concerned additional courses needed. These included advanced management courses, better mathematics courses, and smaller classes. Also mentioned were courses for developing leadership and decision-making processes; job interviews and how to prepare resumes; more quantitative and computer courses; greater variety and greater specialization in courses; more and better management courses; expanding offerings in accounting and finance; and courses in taxes and insurance, personnel and labor relations, hospital administration, and small business management.

Some students expressed a desire for more electives from which to choose with fewer required majors. Some of them wanted greater freedom to construct their own schedules, also suggesting more extensive student involvement in faculty evaluation.

Faculty Recommendations

The importance of more internship programs was mentioned frequently by faculty members. One faculty member recommended a wider range of courses taught by actual specialists in the various fields. Some respondents mentioned the need for more communication with the business community, suggesting that faculty members should participate in the activities of the business community.

A few faculty members mentioned the importance of proper staffing, indicating the need for a higher quality of teaching. By the same token, one faculty member recommended recruiting students of a higher quality. Another respondent recommended a larger budget for the faculty, urging higher salaries ostensibly as a means of upgrading the faculty. To improve student quality, one faculty member recommended using a minimum cumulative grade point average as an admission requirement.

Some of the recommendations made were in the area of quantitative courses and computerization. Needed was more quantitative course equipment such as keypunch machines and more support personnel such as secretaries. A number of the respondents recommended courses in computer-assisted instruction and computerized accounting, with simulation programs in purchasing, receiving, inventory, accounts payable/receivable, and payroll.

One faculty member recommended more extensive counseling and placement services. Another recommended a better and more formal approach to advising students.

Several faculty members recommended placing greater emphasis on communication skills, such as report writing. Others recommended greater emphasis on the arts, business ethics, values, leadership, and research techniques.

Other recommendations concerned more comprehensive course offerings. Some faculty members opted for more electives, while others wanted more required courses and more rigorous concentration, as well as a greater variety of courses. For one faculty member, this broader base would include courses in remedial reading and self-motivation.

Alumni Recommendations

Many of the alumni's recommendations concerned programs more relevant to the business world. One alumnus cited the need for firsthand experience, not just classroom experience. Many alumni were referring to cooperative education of the internship kind. They emphasized the need for showing students how business actually works through the medium of personal observation. For them, classroom experience ought to include more speakers from the actual business community. The emphasis on day-to-day business activities would, presumably, lead to a study of "more realistic, everyday problems of the business world rather than case studies where students assume the role of president." Another alumnus pointed out that most employers want experience plus a college degree, not the other way around.

Some alumni commented that the courses they had themselves taken were too theoretical, contending that courses should emphasize specific skills more than they do. One cited the need for technically oriented courses because "that's where the jobs are, and management is not impressed by fancy education or theories . . . everybody has to start at the bottom." Some respondents preferred the case-study method as a means for becoming more realistic and practical. Courses in communication, including better writing, speaking, and interpersonal relationships, were stressed by a number of the alumni.

Recommendations were also made with respect to counseling. Better faculty advice concerning job-placement information and job opportunities was recommended. Some alumni felt that professors are too busy and too uninterested. One alumnus said that he is a welder on an assembly line "going nowhere, just as 90 percent of those who graduated with me."

Some alumni suggested that a larger number of advanced courses, as in management theory, be offered. Others, however, claimed that such courses would only be training students for levels they would never attain in the business world. A number of the alumni favored more individualized instruction; more computer courses; courses about career development, job strategies, and sales training; and a larger number of quantitative courses involving data processing and information systems.

One alumnus recommended that students and alumni meet in give-and-take sessions. One recommended a newsletter published four to six times annually in which students could share experience and information about job openings, to name but one possibility. One alumnus summarized the matter particularly well.

> Expand internship/coop opportunities, develop senior level courses in job development strategies or career development, require communication courses (written communication, interpersonal communication, and speech communication), better student-advisor relationships should be developed, and better placement opportunities should be developed. Also, students should have the opportunity to be involved with the business community before graduation. Students could be given the opportunity to observe someone in the proposed career for a certain length of time in order for them to become aware of the job role and responsibilities. There should be more development of student/business community organizations.

Business Manager Recommendations

The major recommendations made by the business managers concerned the practical business aspect of education. The idea of internship-cooperative programs was mentioned by most of the managers. Their emphasis was on work-study and field experience.

They stressed practicality and the real business world, especially how a firm really operates in its own political environment. On-the-job training was recommended as a way of placing students in closer touch with the real business world.

The implications of these recommendations are clear. Classes should simulate the actual business situation more closely, being less theoretical and more practical. Instructors should have more practical business experience and emphasize case work and problem solving.

Many of the business managers believed that courses in communication are needed, especially ones covering basic reading and writing skills. Some of them thought that a better balance with the humanities and social sciences should be maintained.

One manager mentioned the need for career counseling. Another pointed out the need for "learning how to learn."

A number of managers were interested in the provision of more specialized courses, especially in the areas of computer technology, retailing, management information, data communications, and data-processing technology. The comments of one business manager are particularly noteworthy.

> The skills that we need in our business are so specialized that we can't—don't—expect any business administration college program to teach them. Rather, we look for students who are intelligent, understand how our company (or any company) functions, how functions integrate, how to communicate, and how to solve problems and to plan. We want students who can think practically. With those very basic—but essential—qualifications, any person—BA major or fine arts major—can meet our company needs very well, and can enjoy a very successful career in business management.

SUMMARY OF RESULTS

Out of 450 questionnaires sent out, 206 were returned and usable, the rate of return ranging from 33 percent for students to 72 percent for faculty members. The sample was male by a ratio of about 2:1. A decided majority of the students were career oriented and planned to continue studies connected with business. The faculty members had a fairly good background both of teaching

experience and of previous connections with the business world.
Most of the alumni were more or less recent graduates involved in
many different lines of business. As a group, they had found employment in a variety of ways, with no one method prevailing. The
business firms represented a good cross section of both small and
large firms. A majority of the firms were in manufacturing, with
the remaining firms representing many other kinds of business activities. Like the alumni, the business managers had obtained employment in a variety of ways, with no single means predominating.

As concerned the purpose of business administration studies,
all four groups were only moderately in agreement with the idea
that such studies should prepare students for a specific job, whether
in business or elsewhere. While all four groups contended that
business programs ought to help students define personal goals,
faculty members and alumni were significantly more in favor of
this purpose than were students or business managers. Students
and alumni were strongly in favor of business programs that prepare students directly for their fields of study; more so than faculty
members and business managers, who favored this purpose only
mildly.

All four groups were strongly in favor of programs helping
students explore career opportunities, and all believed that the
programs prepared students for better positions than might otherwise be available to them. The alumni were greatly in favor of
programs assisting students in finding full-time positions, with the
other three groups being only mildly in favor of this purpose. All
four groups were strongly in favor of programs that develop career
understanding and explore career opportunities, with faculty members and alumni registering quite high on the first purpose and
students, faculty members, and alumni very high on the latter purpose. All four groups were strongly in favor of programs helping
students develop professional attitudes and perspectives, teaching
communication skills (getting along with supervisors, subordinates,
and colleagues), and strengthening students' self-confidence. More
than the other three groups, business managers favored programs
helping students find their self-identities. Finally, all four groups
were thoroughly in agreement that the programs ought to help students develop leadership potential.

In the matter of program determinants, all four groups were
either mildly or strongly in agreement with the idea that the business administration faculty is in a good position to help determine
what subject matter should be taught in business courses. All four
groups were slightly more pronounced in their belief that the

business community is in such a position. However, the business managers disagreed very definitely with letting students make such decisions, with the students themselves being uncertain and faculty members and alumni favoring the idea only mildly.

In the case of admission criteria, faculty members and alumni were far more strongly than students or business managers in favor of admitting students on the basis of typical criteria (grade point average, faculty recommendations, entrance examinations, and counselor and/or school administrator opinions). None of the four groups favored selecting students on the basis of business administration faculty judgment alone or student judgment alone. Faculty members were particularly opposed to using student judgment as a decision criterion.

Turning to the internship–cooperative experience, all four groups favored such a program, especially students and alumni. While the alumni, business managers, and students all believed that such a program would be very helpful in realizing business administration program objectives, faculty members tended to register uncertainty.

As for the role of the business administration faculty, the students believed that it ought to provide vocational career counseling, with the other three groups being somewhat uncertain regarding this function. The students, alumni, and business managers were strongly in support of using the faculty to help students select suitable courses, with faculty members supporting this function only in a lukewarm fashion. Regarding a possible liaison between faculty members and the business community, faculty members did not support the idea even tepidly, students were somewhat supportive, and business managers and alumni were decidedly strong in their support.

With respect to the vocational relevance of business administration programs, all four groups considered the programs of good quality and quite relevant.

Turning to the adequacy of the program in preparing students for jobs, faculty members, alumni, and business managers all believed that the programs prepare students for jobs that would otherwise not be available to them and that graduates of the programs are better prepared for the business world than are graduates of nonbusiness programs.

A large majority of the students had business careers in mind and did not regret enrolling in business administration programs. Although fewer than half of the students believed that their programs were preparing them well for graduate studies or that such programs had helped them choose a suitable career path, a large majority would recommend their programs to other students; 62 percent of the students evaluated their programs as good, 17 percent as excellent.

Those faculty members, alumni, and business managers who rated business programs as inadequate listed some of their reasons for doing so. Faculty members' statements included the beliefs that other schools, such as liberal arts schools, prepare students for the business world equally well; that some business graduates cannot spell or write; and that these students ought to spend more time in the liberal arts. Alumni's statements included the beliefs that the market is saturated with business majors; that schools teach too much theory, whereas the crying need is for practicality; that more internship-cooperative programs are needed; and that business administration programs should offer more concentrated and specialized training. Business managers' statements included the beliefs that a degree is of secondary importance compared to practical business experience; that liberal arts students can be trained just as easily as business school graduates for many positions; and that more emphasis is needed on individual skills, goals, motivation, and specialized training.

Finally, the members of all four groups were asked to recommend changes they personally would like to see made in business administration programs. The primary concerns of students were with the need for better and more relevant instruction presented by instructors conversant with the actual world of business. They expressed a need for more practice and less theory and for greater concern with the real world of business, especially through the medium of internship-cooperative programs, highly recommended by students. The students wanted less lecturing and more discussion, more course work in communication skills of all kinds, career counseling, smaller classes, and a larger number of quantitative courses including data processing and information systems. Some students cited the need for more electives, flexibility in scheduling, fewer required majors, and a voice in evaluating the faculty.

Like the students, the faculty members recommended the greater use of internship-cooperative programs, although not as frequently. The faculty members were keenly aware of the need for greater contact with actual specialists and with the business community. They were also concerned with standards such as minimum grade point averages for improving the quality of students admitted. More courses in the quantitative area were recommended by a number of faculty members. Many of them were aware of the need for more effective teaching, counseling, career study, and placement. Also mentioned were the need for improving communication skills and more varied course offerings, including courses in remedial reading and self-motivation.

Much of the alumni's concern was in the area of program relevance to the world of business. They advocated more first-hand experience for students beyond mere classroom experience. Recommended were internship-cooperative programs, speakers from the actual business community, and showing students the actual, day-to-day operations of business firms. Alumni pointed out that employers prefer experience to a college degree and that courses are often too theoretical and unrealistic. Many alumni preferred the case-study approach, as well as courses in communication that include reading, writing, speaking, and interpersonal relationships. A number of alumni recommended more effective counseling with respect to job placement and greater faculty interest in students. Many of them favored courses in the quantitative area involving computers, data processing, and information systems. One alumnus recommended a newsletter in which both students and alumni would participate.

The concerns of business managers were mostly with the practical business aspect of education. Their emphasis was on work-study, field experience, and internship-cooperative programs. How a firm actually functions and on-the-job training were mentioned frequently. The managers recommended that faculty members have a greater amount of practical business experience and that classes invite representatives of the business community to speak. Communication skills were emphasized, particularly basic reading and writing skills. Career counseling and "learning how to learn" were also stressed. One manager advocated a better balance for business programs by including the humanities and social sciences. Managers emphasized quantitative courses, especially ones dealing with computer technology, data communications, data-processing technology, and management information. Several managers were particularly emphatic in stating that more important for students than coming to a firm "ready-made" and specialized was being intelligent, understanding how a company functions, communicating, problem solving, and planning. Students capable of thinking practically are more important than students merely possessing a degree.

5

CONCLUSIONS, RECOMMENDATIONS, AND SUMMARY

CONCLUSIONS

Of the new courses now finding their way into the business curriculum, the most valuable ones, in the opinion of the sample members, are in the areas of communication and quantitative methods. Of the various program innovations, the sample found internship-cooperative programs of special significance.

While it cannot be concluded from the study that liberal arts should be the foundation of a business education, the sample provided definite evidence indicating that there are specific liberal-arts factors of special importance to business organizations and that these factors are even more important than is a good business education. In addition to communication skills, business managers value individuals with general intelligence, capable of problem solving and planning. These are liberal-arts skills without which a business degree is of little value in the view of many managers.

The questionnaire part of the study reaffirmed the importance of a real-world orientation toward business, if business education programs are to be successful. As important as issues such as the core curriculum may be, the study sample recognized other, more urgent issues such as internship-cooperative programs, teaching methods, counseling, communication, the need for quantitative courses, and emphasis on a business world orientation toward practicality.

Some of the sample members pointed out that business organizations value experience more than academic degrees and that business administration programs typically immerse students in highly theoretical problems involving levels of management that they are unlikely ever to attain. It is possible to conclude that business curricula need to be reevaluated, relating them more effectively to the actual world of business.

The most urgent needs seem to be at opposite ends of the educational spectrum: one, a general liberal-arts orientation; the other, a highly specialized orientation. The need for humanistic and social intelligence is obvious from the remarks of the business managers included in the sample, as is the need for broadly conceived communication skills. On the other hand, managers look to those who have specialized in some particular area such as computer technology to perform functions transcending ordinary, common sense routine. The need for a series of courses producing a trained specialist with sufficient competence and experience to assume a technician's role supersedes any formal debate concerning the pros and cons of a core curriculum.

It is of interest to note that not one member of the sample ever mentioned the need to be familiar with modern management theory. This omission raises the issue of the relevance of the Master of Business Administration degree and, to a certain extent, of management theory itself. The managers of the sample seemed to believe that management is essentially a matter of technical knowledge, adding a certain humanistic and social common sense, provided that the individual is sufficiently capable, with capability something other than a talent provided simply by formal training.

The problem of competency-based evaluation surfaced only indirectly in the questionnaire study. Only one student mentioned the importance of having students evaluate instructors. Yet, many students felt that instructors were not sufficiently competent in certain ways, as in lacking business experience, interest in students, or interest in the subject matter. Business managers evidently believed that their present methods of evaluation were adequate and that no venture into new programs of performance-based evaluation was needed. College faculty members likewise displayed no particular concern about making student admission

criteria more stringent. None of the four groups appeared interested in embarking on systematic evaluation systems. Encouraging quality education through a competency-oriented, performance-
based, systematic approach to evaluating instruction seems very
unlikely.

If, indeed, the job market is glutted with unemployed business majors, then one solution is the one recommended by the
sample members: greater program relevance to the needs of the
business community. Both the alumni and the business managers
of the study sample noted that students seem to have an unrealistic
perception of the business organization, a perception gleaned primarily from textbook cases. However, the danger always exists
of producing individuals excessively specialized and narrow-minded
with respect to the business world. Even though much of the first
two years of a good business administration program may be
useless in terms of its immediate applicability, its long-run value
may be inestimable, becoming obvious much later when the student
may already be in graduate school or trying to understand more
clearly the workings of the corporation for which he works. What
business calls career education may involve the need to absorb a
great variety of studies as complex as the typical liberal-arts
program. Today's highly complex scene requires the business
student to be acquainted with corporate structure, corruption, the
law, consumerism, quantitative technology, and a foreign language,
to name but a few topics.

RECOMMENDATIONS

The results of the study do not point to any one specific optimum model or program generally recommendable to schools of
business administration. However, the recommendations made by
the four study groups can be heartily seconded as a set of useful
guidelines. These include, first, the need for more internship-
cooperative programs and for more student participation in such
programs.

Second, curricula and teaching methods must be improved
by downplaying theory and placing greater emphasis on practice;
lecturing less and discussing more; relying more on case studies;
having smaller clases; employing instructors with considerable,
practical business experience; and inviting more lecturers from
the business community to speak.

Third, students need more firsthand experience with the business world through field experience, work-study, and on-the-job training and a greater awareness of the nature of the business world, including its emphasis on experience, communication, and knowledge of a firm's mode of operation. Textbook make-believe cases provide an intellectual exercise that fails miserably to attune students to the actual world of business.

Fourth, faculty members must exhibit more concern for the welfare of students. More career counseling is needed. Faculty members should be more willing to advise students as to which courses to take and what career possibilities exist. Students must be made more aware of job opportunities and offered more in the way of job placement services.

Fifth, students must be better prepared in the area of communication. For some of them, this means much more rigorous training in the basics of reading, writing, and speaking. For most, it means a special study of the human-relations skills implicit in the humanities and the social sciences. A good liberal-arts background will help satisfy this need.

Sixth, more opportunities should be made available for students to enroll in and specialize in quantitative courses. Automation is here and is expected to continue proliferating, as will computer technology. Students hould have an opportunity to specialize early in an area of data processing technology, if they so desire.

A seventh recommendation concerns the dilemma posed by the need both for specialization and for a broad background including survey courses in business and the liberal arts. In addition to a broadly based Bachelor of Arts degree in business administration, certificates of specialization could be offered. In this way, an employer could more reliably introduce new graduates into specialized areas of his business even though they had only Bachelor of Arts degrees. Students might, as a result, become less uncertain of their employability in the existing job market.

The first seven recommendations of the study were based on the questionnaire results. Three more recommendations were made on the basis of considerations growing out of the literature review and the questionnaire data.

An eighth recommendation was based on the perceived need for business administration students to have a deeper awareness of the social, psychological, and other situational components of management. It is recommended that business students be made more knowledgeable concerning the conceptual framework of modern management theory. The important concepts include systems theory, action research, management by objectives, organization development, communication and creativity, release of individual potential, participation concepts, and managing the new generation. Business students should be made more fully aware of the historical and economic factors that underlie the various social and psychological characteristics of the modern-day employee in the United States.

A ninth recommendation was motivated by the Japanese management success story. It is recommended that business students should be made aware of management problems and their solution in the context of other cultures. Such cross-cultural studies should be more than merely academic exercises. By taking a good look at how the Japanese, for example, resolve their management problems, students of the U.S. scene will be better able to take a good look at themselves. If there exists too much selfishness and lack of responsible commitment to group welfare in the U.S. work scene, it will be more likely driven home through observing other systems than through formal studies that often, by their very nature, mask the psychological and ethical realities underlying an impressive intellectual format.

Finally, a tenth recommendation is that the present study be replicated using larger and more diverse sample populations. In particular, it is recommended that future study samples include sizable numbers of adult or evening school students who are likely to be participating in nontraditional and off-campus programs of business education.

SUMMARY

The purpose of this study was to find ways and means for improving business administration programs. The problem of the study was that of establishing guidelines for making meaningful decisions concerning curricula and special emphases in collegiate business administration programs. The study sought to formulate these guidelines through the medium of an in-depth review of the literature relevant to the specified problem and on the basis of an empirical study of responses from four concerned groups: students in undergraduate business administration programs, faculty members teaching courses in such programs, alumni of schools offering such programs, and the business community.

The target population consisted of students, faculty members, alumni, and business organization managers from the states of Massachusetts and Rhode Island; 10 colleges were involved. A total of 206 usable questionnaires was secured from the 450 individuals sampled. The response rate was 33 percent for the 200 students, 72 percent for the 50 faculty members, 51 percent for the 100 alumni, and 54 percent for the 100 business managers.

Each questionnaire asked the individual to respond on several kinds of scales to various statements concerning business administration programs. The respondents were also asked to explain their reasons for certain of their answers and to recommend changes in business administration programs. The data gathered were used to answer nine specific research questions.

1. There was considerable agreement on the part of all four groups concerning the purposes of business administration programs. All four groups were strongly in favor of programs emphasizing career understanding and development; helping students develop professional attitudes and perspectives; strengthening student self-confidence; teaching communication skills (reading, writing, speaking, and getting along with others); and developing leadership potential. All four groups were moderately in agreement with the idea that business programs ought to prepare students for specific jobs and help students define personal goals. Students and alumni strongly favored programs that prepare students directly for some field of study—something faculty members and business managers were only lukewarm in favoring. The alumni strongly favored programs helping students find full-time positions, while the other three groups favored this purpose only mildly. Much more than the other three groups, business managers favored programs helping students find themselves.

2. As regarded program determinants, all four groups believed that both faculty members and the business community should be permitted a significant input into curriculum determination. Business managers were definitely opposed to letting students decide program content, and even the students themselves were uncertain regarding this privilege, with faculty members and alumni favoring it only mildly.

3. None of the four groups favored admitting students on the basis either of faculty or of student judgment alone. Faculty members and alumni, far more than students or business managers, favored using the usual criteria such as grade point averages,

faculty recommendations, entrance examinations, and counselor and/or school administrator opinions.

4. The sample as a whole believed that faculty members should be considerably more active in counseling, especially in the matter of career decisions and job placement. Many sample members believed that the faculty should be more effective in vocational career counseling and in advising students concerning course selections. Special emphasis was placed on the importance of faculty members working more closely with the business community.

5. As for the vocational relevance of business administration programs, all four groups considered the programs of good quality and quite relevant.

6. All four groups believed that the programs prepare students for jobs that would otherwise not be available to them and that business graduates are better prepared for the business world than are graduates of nonbusiness schools.

7. All four groups believed that internship-cooperative programs are of special importance, with students, alumni, and business managers placing great emphasis on such programs.

8. The overall evaluation of business administration programs by the four groups was quite good. Of the students, 62 percent rated their programs as good, 17 percent as excellent. While fewer than half of the students believed that their programs were preparing them well for graduate studies or that they had helped them choose suitable careers, almost 75 percent of the students stated that they would recommend their programs to other students.

9. Despite the overall high support for existing business programs, a number of significant criticisms and recommendations for change were made. The most common criticisms voiced were that business school graduates are often unable to write or to spell; the market is saturated with business majors; business schools teach too much theory, whereas what is needed is practicality; experience is more important than a degree; other schools, such as liberal-arts schools, can prepare students equally well for the business world; schools do not train students adequately for the needs of the business world, and more specialization is needed in the various business programs; insufficient emphasis is placed on individual skills, goals, motivation, and specialized training; and there is insufficient emphasis on internship-cooperative programs.

The most frequently made recommendations concerned internship-cooperative programs, curricula and teaching methods, a business-community or real-world orientation, counseling, communication, and quantitative methods courses.

Internship-Cooperative programs: Probably the single most agreed-upon recommendation was for establishing internship-cooperative programs. Except for the faculty members, all groups valued such programs highly, as a means of improving current business administration programs.

Curricula and teaching methods: Numerous criticisms attacked the excessively theoretical approach of many business administration courses. Recommendations included reducing lectures and increasing discussions and case studies, as well as reducing class sizes. Typical recommendations were to the effect that instructors should have previous business experience and that more lecturers be representatives of the business community. Many students commented that there were simply not enough instructors.

Business world orientation: Many respondents believed that instructors were not familiar enough with the actual world of business to which instruction ought to be extremely relevant. Business managers cited the need for more firsthand experience of business outside mere classroom experience. Some alumni pointed out that courses are often too theoretical and unrealistic, and that employers prefer experience and individual competence to college degrees. Various managers emphasized the importance of field experience, work-study, and on-the-job training. Many respondents believed that students were not adequately aware of the realities of the business world, especially as concerned social structure, communication, and the role of experience.

Counseling: Students and alumni were pronounced in believing that faculty members frequently displayed insufficient concern for students. All four groups favored counseling geared to career exploration and job placement. Students wanted more help in selecting courses.

Communication: All four groups agreed that it was necessary to prepare students more effectively in the area of communication: not only in reading, writing, and speaking, but also in human-relations skills. Some sample members wanted better student backgrounds in the humanities and the social sciences. One alumnus recommended a newsletter to improve student-alumnus communication.

Quantitative courses: All four groups were decidedly of the opinion that more should be done in the quantitative area than currently is being done in business administration programs. Recommended most were courses in computer technology, data communications, management information, and data-processing technology.

Appendix A: Geographic Study Locations

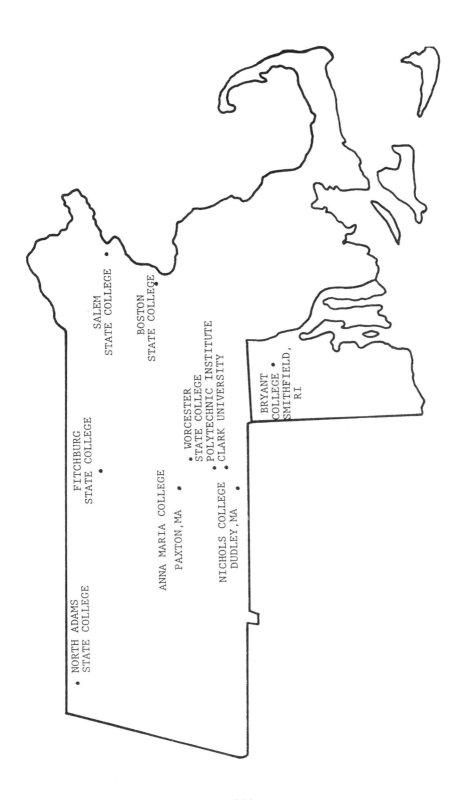

NORTH ADAMS
STATE COLLEGE

FITCHBURG
STATE COLLEGE

SALEM
STATE COLLEGE

BOSTON
STATE COLLEGE

ANNA MARIA COLLEGE
PAXTON, MA

WORCESTER
STATE COLLEGE
POLYTECHNIC INSTITUTE
CLARK UNIVERSITY

NICHOLS COLLEGE
DUDLEY, MA

BRYANT
COLLEGE
SMITHFIELD,
RI

Appendix B: Transmittal Letter and Questionnaire for Junior and Senior Students

DEPARTMENT OF MANAGEMENT

January 22, 1980

Dear_____:

  I am currently engaged in an important study designed to provide guidelines for changing and improving collegiate business administration programs. In connection with that study, I have constructed a special questionnaire. Your cooperation in filling out and returning the questionnaire will sincerely be appreciated.

  An expected major outcome of the study will be a model business administration program reflecting the input of students majoring in business administration, college faculty members teaching business administration courses, alumni of schools of business administration, and business firms that have been employing graduates of business administration schools. When the study has been completed, its results will be made available to you upon request. These results may prove to be most interesting to you and other business administration students.

  Please return the completed questionnaire and "Informed Consent" form within the next seven (7) days, in the enclosed stamped, self-addressed envelope. You are guaranteed complete confidentiality and anonymity.

       Sincerely yours,

       Donald L. Joyal
       Professor of Organizational
        Behavior and Management
       Associate Department Chairman

DLJ:zq

QUESTIONNAIRE

SECTION A

DIRECTIONS: Please answer each question by checking (√) the space corresponding to your choice.

_____

1. Sex:

_____ Male   _____ Female

2. How long have you been pursuing a business administration program?

_____ (1) One year

_____ (2) Two years

_____ (3) Three years

_____ (4) Four years

3. What do you intend to do after finishing the business administration program in which you are currently enrolled?

_____ Seek full-time employment in the field of business administration

_____ Begin full-time graduate study of business administration

_____ Work full-time in order to attend graduate business administration school part-time

_____ Relocate to another part of the United States

_____ Join the Armed Forces

_____ Remain in my present position, irrespective of its nature

_____ I am still undecided about my future plans

_____ Other (specify): _____

114

4. Why did you choose the business administration program in which you are currently enrolled? (Check as many reasons as apply).

_____ (1) There are many good jobs available related to my field of study.

_____ (2) My college offered no other programs of interest to me.

_____ (3) The business administration program was recommended to me by other persons.

_____ (4) I wish to develop specific skills currently in obvious demand.

_____ (5) I had no special reason for choosing this program.

_____ (6) Other reasons (specify): _____

==

SECTION B

DIRECTIONS: Please indicate the extent to which you agree or disagree with the statements listed below describing business administration programs. Next to each statement, place a check mark ($\sqrt{}$) in that category representing your opinion. Your answers are to indicate what you believe business administration programs ought to be like, not what they currently are like.

PART I. THE PURPOSE OF BUSI- NESS ADMINISTRATION PROGRAMS OUGHT TO BE TO:	Agree Strongly	Agree	Am Uncertain	Disagree	Disagree Strongly
5. Prepare students for employment but not necessarily in the field of business administration					
6. Assist students in defining their personal goals					
7. Prepare students for positions related directly to their field of study					

115

	Agree Strongly	Agree	Am Uncertain	Disagree	Disagree Strongly
8. Help students investigate career opportunities related to their field of study	___	___	___	___	___
9. Prepare students for better positions than those which might otherwise be available to them	___	___	___	___	___
10. Help students find full-time employment	___	___	___	___	___
11. Assist students in developing job values	___	___	___	___	___
12. Provide students with a better understanding of what careers they wish to pursue	___	___	___	___	___
13. Develop both basic and advanced skills in the chosen area of study	___	___	___	___	___
14. Help students develop the attitudes and perspectives they need to do well in positions related to their chosen fields	___	___	___	___	___
15. Teach the communication skills involved in getting along with superiors, subordinates, and colleagues	___	___	___	___	___
16. Strengthen student vocational self-confidence	___	___	___	___	___
17. Help students find themselves	___	___	___	___	___
18. Assist students in developing leadership potential	___	___	___	___	___

	Agree Strongly	Agree	Am Uncertain	Disagree	Disagree Strongly

PART II. BUSINESS ADMINISTRATION
          PROGRAM DETERMINANTS

19. The business administra-
    tion faculty is qualified
    to help determine what
    courses to each in busi-
    ness administration
    programs

20. The business community is
    qualified to help deter-
    mine what courses should
    be taught in business
    administration programs

21. The students enrolled
    in business administra-
    tion programs are quali-
    fied to help determine what
    courses should be taught
    in business administra-
    tion programs

PART III. ADMISSION CRITERIA

22. The admission of students
    into business administra-
    tion programs should be
    determined by the students
    themselves: they know best
    whether or not they are
    suited for such programs

23. The admission of students
    into business administra-
    tion programs should be
    based on previous school
    grade point averages, the re-
    commendations of faculty
    members, counselors, and
    school administrators,
    entrance examinations,
    and/or other personal
    documentation

	Agree Strongly	Agree	Am Uncertain	Disagree	Disagree Strongly
24. The admission of students into business administration programs should largely be the responsibility of the business administration faculty	_____	____	_____	_____	_____

PART IV. INTERNSHIP/COOPERATIVE EXPERIENCES

25. The business internship/ cooperative program within a business administration curriculum ought to be an integral part of a student's learning experience	_____	____	_____	_____	_____
26. The business internship/ cooperative positions that students secure while enrolled in business administration programs are essential in meeting the objectives of those programs	_____	____	_____	_____	_____

PART V. THE FUNCTION OF THE BUSINESS ADMINISTRATION FACULTY

27. A primary function of the business administration faculty ought to be to provide business administration students with vocational career counseling	_____	____	_____	_____	_____
28. A primary function of the business administration faculty ought to be to counsel/advise students in selecting courses	_____	____	_____	_____	_____
29. A primary function of the business administration faculty ought to be to work closely with the business community	_____	____	_____	_____	_____

Please answer each question by checking (√) the space next to your choice. Unless you are specifically asked to do otherwise, choose the one answer reflecting your opinion most accurately.

30. Why did you enroll in a business administration program? Place check marks (√) next to all appropriate answers.

_____ (1) My career goal is to enter some aspect of business administration.

_____ (2) I want to acquire knowledge that will prepare me very directly to enter the world of work.

_____ (3) The program was recommended by my high school guidance counselor.

_____ (4) Someone in my family majored in business administration while in college and is now successful in business.

_____ (5) Other (specify): _____

31. If you had to choose a college program again, would you enroll in a business administration program?

_____ (1) Yes

_____ (2) No

_____ (3) I don't know

32. Do you believe that the program in which you are enrolled is preparing you to assume responsibilities related to your field of study?

_____ (1) Yes

_____ (2) No

_____ (3) I don't know

33. Do you believe that your program is doing a good job of preparing you for graduate studies?

_____ (1) Yes

_____ (2) No

_____ (3) I don't know

34. Has your program helped you select a career path for yourself?

_____ (1) Yes

_____ (2) No

_____ (3) I don't know

35. Would you recommend the program in which you are enrolled to other students?

_____ (1) Yes

_____ (2) No

_____ (3) I don't know

36. On the whole, how would you rate the quality of the business administration program at your college?

_____ (1) Excellent

_____ (2) Good

_____ (3) Fair

_____ (4) Poor

37. How would you rate the business administration instruction that you have received?

_____ (1) Excellent

_____ (2) Good

_____ (3) Fair

_____ (4) Poor

SECTION D

DIRECTIONS: Discuss briefly your opinions concerning the following
question.

38. What changes would you make in the curriculum of your business administration program in order to increase its value as a learning experience?

_____

_____

_____

_____

_____

_____

_____

_____

_____

_____

_____

_____

Appendix C:
Transmittal Letter
and Questionnaire
for Business
Administration Program
Faculty Members

DEPARTMENT OF MANAGEMENT

January 22, 1980

Dear _____ :

      I am currently engaged in an important study designed to provide guidelines for changing and improving collegiate business administration programs. In connection with that study, I have constructed a special questionnaire. Your cooperation in filling out and returning the questionnaire will sincerely be appreciated.

      An expected major outcome of the study will be a model business administration program reflecting the input of students majoring in business administration, college faculty members teaching business administration courses, alumni of schools of business administration, and business firms that have been employing graduates of business administration schools. When the study has been completed, its results will be made available to you upon request. These results may prove to be most interesting to you and other business administration program faculty members.

      Please return the completed questionnaire and "Informed Consent" form within the next seven (7) days, in the enclosed stamped, self-addressed envelope. You are guaranteed complete confidentiality and anonymity.

Sincerely yours,

Donald L. Joyal
Professor of Organizational
   Behavior and Management
Associate Department Chairman

DLJ:zq

QUESTIONNAIRE

SECTION A

<u>DIRECTIONS</u>: Please answer each question by checking (√) the space
corresponding to your choice.

---

1. Sex:

    _____ Male

    _____ Female

2. How many years have you been teaching?

    _____ (1) Fewer than three years

    _____ (2) Between three and six years

    _____ (3) More than six years

3. What were you doing just before you joined the business administration
   faculty?

    _____ (1) Worked in an occupation related to business administration

    _____ (2) Taught college business administration courses at another
              institution

    _____ (3) Taught at the secondary-school level

    _____ (4) Other (specify): _____

SECTION B

<u>DIRECTIONS</u>: Please indicate the extent to which you agree or disagree
with the statements listed below describing business administration programs. Next to each statement, place a check mark
(√) in that category representing your opinion. Your answers
are to indicate what you believe business administration
programs ought to be like, <u>not</u> what they currently are like.

PART I. THE PURPOSE OF BUSI- NESS ADMINISTRATION PROGRAMS OUGHT TO BE TO:	Agree Strongly	Agree	Am Uncertain	Disagree	Disagree Strongly
4. Prepare students for employment, but not necessarily in the field of business administration	_____	_____	_____	_____	_____
5. Prepare students for positions related directly to their field of study	_____	_____	_____	_____	_____
6. Assist students in defining their personal goals	_____	_____	_____	_____	_____
7. Help students investigate career opportunities related to their field of study	_____	_____	_____	_____	_____
8. Prepare students for better positions than those which might otherwise be available to them	_____	_____	_____	_____	_____
9. Help students find full-time employment	_____	_____	_____	_____	_____
10. Assist students in developing job values	_____	_____	_____	_____	_____
11. Provide students with a better understanding of what careers they wish to pursue	_____	_____	_____	_____	_____
12. Develop both basic and advanced skills in the chosen area of study	_____	_____	_____	_____	_____
13. Help students develop the attitudes and perspectives they need to do well in positions related to their chosen fields	_____	_____	_____	_____	_____
14. Teach the communication skills involved in getting along with superiors, subordinates, and colleagues	_____	_____	_____	_____	_____

	Agree Strongly	Agree	Am Uncertain	Disagree	Disagree Strongly
15. Strengthen student vocational self-confidence	_____	____	_____	_____	_____
16. Help students find themselves	_____	____	_____	_____	_____
17. Assist students in developing leadership potential	_____	____	_____	_____	_____

II. BUSINESS ADMINISTRATION PROGRAM DETERMINANTS

18. The business administration faculty is qualified to help determine what courses to teach in business administration programs	_____	____	_____	_____	_____
19. The business community is qualified to help determine what courses should be taught in business administration programs	_____	____	_____	_____	_____
20. The students enrolled in business administration programs are qualified to help determine what courses should be taught in business administration programs	_____	____	_____	_____	_____

PART III. ADMISSION CRITERIA

21. The admission of students into business administration programs should be based on previous school grade point averages, the recommendations of faculty members, counselors, and school administrators, entrance examinations, and/or other personal documentation	_____	____	_____	_____	_____

128

	Agree Strongly	Agree	Am Uncertain	Disagree	Disagree Strongly
22. The admission of students into business administration programs should be largely the responsibility of the business administration faculty	_____	_____	_____	_____	_____
23. The admission of students into business administration programs should be determined by the students themselves: they know best whether or not they are suited for such programs	_____	_____	_____	_____	_____

PART IV: INTERNSHIP/COOPERATIVE
          EXPERIENCES

24. The business internship/ cooperative program within a business administration curriculum ought to be an integral part of a student's learning experience	_____	_____	_____	_____	_____
25. The business internship/ cooperative positions that students secure while enrolled in business administration programs are essential in meeting the objectives of those programs	_____	_____	_____	_____	_____

PART V: THE FUNCTION OF THE BUSINESS
         ADMINISTRATION FACULTY

26. A primary function of the business administration faculty ought to be to provide business administration students with vocational career counseling	_____	_____	_____	_____	_____

	Agree Strongly	Agree	Am Uncertain	Disagree	Disagree Strongly
27. A primary function of the business administration faculty ought to be to counsel/advise students in selecting courses	___	___	___	___	___
28. A primary function of the business administration faculty ought to be to work closely with the business community	___	___	___	___	___

SECTION C

DIRECTIONS: Please answer each question by checking (✓) the space next to your choice. Unless you are specifically asked to do otherwise, choose the one answer reflecting your opinion most accurately.

29. Do you believe that business administration programs are preparing students for jobs for which they could not otherwise qualify?

_____ (1) Yes

_____ (2) No

_____ (3) I don't know

30. In your opinion, are graduates of business administration programs better prepared for the business world than are students graduating from nonbusiness degree programs?

_____ (1) Yes

_____ (2) No

_____ (3) I don't know

31. If you answered "NO" to questions #29 and/or #30, please indicate your reasons below.

_____

_____

_____

_____

_____

_____

_____

_____

32. To what extent do you believe that business administration programs help students satisfy the requirements they must meet in order to be employed in responsible positions?

_____ (1) Extremely helpful

_____ (2) Helpful

_____ (3) Minimally or not at all helpful

_____ (4) I don't know

33. On the whole, how would you rate the quality of the business administration program in your college?

_____ (1) Excellent

_____ (2) Good

_____ (3) Fair

_____ (4) Poor

34. What changes would you make in the curriculum of your business administration program in order to increase its value as a learning experience?

_____

_____

_____

_____

_____

_____

_____

_____

_____

_____

_____

_____

_____

_____

Appendix D: Transmittal Letter and Questionnaire for Business Administration School Alumni

DEPARTMENT OF MANAGEMENT

January 22, 1980

Dear _____:

      I am currently engaged in an important study designed to provide guidelines for changing and improving collegiate business administration programs. In connection with that study, I have constructed a special questionnaire. Your cooperation in filling out and returning the questionnaire will sincerely be appreciated.

      An expected major outcome of the study will be a model business administration program reflecting the input of students majoring in business administration, college faculty members teaching business administration courses, alumni of schools of business administration, and business firms that have been employing graduates of business administration schools. When the study has been completed, its results will be made available to you upon request. These results may prove to be most interesting to you and other business administration school alumni.

      Please return the completed questionnaire and "Informed Consent" form within the next seven (7) days, in the enclosed stamped, self-addressed envelope. You are guaranteed complete confidentiality and anonymity.

                          Sincerely yours,

                          Donald L. Joyal
                          Professor of Organizational
                              Behavior and Management
                          Associate Department Chairman

DLJ:zq

QUESTIONNAIRE

SECTION A

DIRECTIONS: Please answer each question by checking (√) the space corresponding to your choice.

1. Sex:

_____ Male

_____ Female

2. How many years ago did you graduate from a business administration program?

_____ (1) One year ago or less

_____ (2) Two to three years ago

_____ (3) Four to five years ago

_____ (4) Six or more years ago

3. How would you classify the business establishment employing you?

_____ (1) Manufacturing

_____ (2) Retail establishment

_____ (3) Travel and/or lodging

_____ (4) Other (specify): _____

4. How did you secure your present employment?

_____ (1) Employment agency (either private or state)

_____ (2) Answered advertisement in professional or trade journal

_____ (3) Answered advertisement in local newspaper

_____ (4) Selected in on-campus college recruiting

_____ (5) Referred to organization by an employee

_____ (6) Other (specify): _____

DIRECTIONS: Please indicate the extent to which you agree or disagree with the statements listed below describing business administration programs. Next to each statement, place a check mark (✓) in that category representing your opinion. Your answers are to indicate what you believe business administration programs ought to be like, not what they currently are like.

PART I. THE PURPOSE OF BUSI-NESS ADMINISTRATION PROGRAMS OUGHT TO BE TO:	Agree Strongly	Agree	Am Uncertain	Disagree	Disagree Strongly
5. Prepare students for employment, but not necessarily in the field of business administration					
6. Prepare students for positions related directly to their field of study					
7. Assist students in defining their personal goals					
8. Help students investigate career opportunities related to their field of study					
9. Prepare students for better positions than those which might otherwise be available to them					
10. Help students find full-time employment					
11. Assist students in developing job values					
12. Provide students with a better understanding of what careers they wish to pursue					
13. Develop both basic and advanced skills in the chosen area of study					

	Agree Strongly	Agree	Am Uncertain	Disagree	Disagree Strongly
14. Help students develop the attitudes and perspectives they need to do well in positions related to their chosen fields	_____	_____	_____	_____	_____
15. Teach the communication skills involved in getting along with superiors, sub-ordinates, and colleagues	_____	_____	_____	_____	_____
16. Strengthen student vocational self-confidence	_____	_____	_____	_____	_____
17. Help students find themselves	_____	_____	_____	_____	_____
18. Assist students in developing leadership potential	_____	_____	_____	_____	_____

PART II. BUSINESS ADMINISTRATION
PROGRAM DETERMINANTS

19. The business administration faculty is qualified to help determine what courses to teach in business administration programs	_____	_____	_____	_____	_____
20. The business community is qualified to help determine what courses should be taught in business administration programs	_____	_____	_____	_____	_____
21. The students enrolled in business administration programs are qualified to help determine what courses should be taught in business administration programs	_____	_____	_____	_____	_____

PART III. ADMISSION CRITERIA

	Agree Strongly	Agree	Am Uncertain	Disagree	Disagree Strongly
22. The admission of students into business administration programs should be based on previous school grade point averages, the recommendations of faculty members, counselors, and school administrators, entrance examinations, and/or other personal documentation	_____	_____	_____	_____	_____
23. The admission of students into business administration programs should largely be the responsibility of the business administration faculty	_____	_____	_____	_____	_____
24. The admission of students into business administration programs should be determined by the students themselves: they know best whether or not they are suited for such programs	_____	_____	_____	_____	_____

PART IV: INTERNSHIP/COOPERATIVE EXPERIENCES

25. The business internship/ cooperative program within a business administration curriculum ought to be an integral part of a student's learning experience	_____	_____	_____	_____	_____
26. The business internship/ cooperative positions that students secure while enrolled in business administration programs are essential in meeting the objectives of those programs	_____	_____	_____	_____	_____

139

PART V

THE FUNCTION OF THE
          BUSINESS ADMINISTRATION
          FACULTY

	Agree Strongly	Agree	Am Uncertain	Disagree	Disagree Strongly
27. A primary function of the business administration faculty ought to be to provide business administration students with vocational career counseling	_____	_____	_____	_____	_____
28. A primary function of the business administration faculty ought to be to counsel/advise students in selecting courses	_____	_____	_____	_____	_____
29. A primary function of the business administration faculty ought to be to work closely with the business community	_____	_____	_____	_____	_____

SECTION C

DIRECTIONS: Please answer each question by checking (✓) the space next
            to your choice. Unless you are specifically asked to do
            otherwise, choose the one answer reflecting your opinion
            most accurately.

30. Do you believe that business administration programs are preparing
     students for jobs for which they could not otherwise qualify?

     _____ (1) Yes

     _____ (2) No

     _____ (3) I don't know

31. In your opinion, are graduates of business administration programs better prepared for the business world than are those students from nonbusiness degree programs?

_____ (1) Yes

_____ (2) No

_____ (3) I don't know

SECTION D

32. If you answered "NO" to questions #27 and/or #28, please explain your reasons.

_____

_____

_____

_____

_____

_____

_____

33. To what extent do you believe that business administration programs help students satisfy the requirements they must meet in order to be employed in responsible positions?

_____ (1) Extremely helpful

_____ (2) Helpful

_____ (3) Minimally or not at all helpful

_____ (4) I don't know

34. On the whole, how would you rate the quality of the business administration program in your college?

_____ (1) Excellent

_____ (2) Good

_____ (3) Fair

_____ (4) Poor

35. What changes would you make in the curriculum of the business administration program of the college from which you graduated in order to increase its value as a learning experience?

_____

_____

_____

_____

_____

_____

_____

_____

Appendix E: Transmittal Letter and Questionnaire for Business Organizations

The Commonwealth of Massachusetts

Worcester State College

486 Chandler Street

Worcester 01602

DEPARTMENT OF MANAGEMENT

January 22, 1980

Dear _____ :

     I am currently engaged in an important study designed to provide guidelines for changing and improving collegiate business administration programs. In connection with that study, I have constructed a special questionnaire. Your cooperation in filling out and returning the questionnaire will sincerely be appreciated.

     An expected major outcome of the study will be a model business administration program reflecting the input of students majoring in business administration, college faculty members teaching business administration courses, alumni of schools of business administration, and businss firms that have been employing graduates of business administration schools. When the study has been completed, its results will be available to you upon request. These results may prove to be most interesting to you and other executives of business organizations.

     Please return the completed questionnaire and "Informed Consent" form within the next seven (7) days, in the enclosed stamped, self-addressed envelope. You are guaranteed complete confidentiality and anonymity.

                           Sincerely yours,

                           Donald L. Joyal
                           Professor of Organizational
                             Behavior and Management
                           Associate Department Chairman

DLJ:zq

QUESTIONNAIRE

SECTION A

<u>DIRECTIONS</u>: Please answer each question by checking (√) the space
corresponding to your choice.

1. How many persons does your organization employ?

_____ (1) Fewer than 100 persons

_____ (2) 100 to 300 persons

_____ (3) 300 to 500 persons

_____ (4) 500 or more persons

2. For how many years have you had graduates of business administration
programs working for your company?

_____ (1) One year

_____ (2) Two to three years

_____ (3) Four to five years

_____ (4) Six or more years

3. How would you describe your business establishment?

_____ (1) Manufacturing

_____ (2) Retail establishment

_____ (3) Travel and/or lodging

_____ (4) Other (specify): _____

4. How have business administration graduates generally been hired by your
organization?

_____ (1) Employment agency (private or state)

_____ (2) Through ads in professional or trade journals

_____ (3) Through ads in local newspapers

_____ (4) By means of on-campus college recruiting

_____ (5) Via employee referrals

_____ (6) Other (specify): _____

DIRECTIONS: Please indicate the extent to which you agree or disagree
with the statements listed below describing business administration programs. Next to each statement, place a check mark
(✔) in that category representing your opinion. Your answers
are to indicate what you believe business administration
programs ought to be like, not what they currently are like.

PART I. THE PURPOSE OF BUSI-
NESS ADMINISTRATION PRO-
GRAMS OUGHT TO BE TO:

	Agree Strongly	Agree	Am Uncertain	Disagree	Disagree Strongly
5. Prepare students for employ-ment, but not necessarily in the field of business admin-istration	_____	_____	_____	_____	_____
6. Prepare students for positions related directly to their field of study	_____	_____	_____	_____	_____
7. Assist students in de-fining their personal goals	_____	_____	_____	_____	_____
8. Help students investigate career opportunities re-lated to their field of study	_____	_____	_____	_____	_____
9. Prepare students for better positions than those which might otherwise be avail-able to them	_____	_____	_____	_____	_____
10. Help students find full-time employment	_____	_____	_____	_____	_____
11. Assist students in developing job values	_____	_____	_____	_____	_____
12. Provide students with a better understanding of what careers they wish to pursue	_____	_____	_____	_____	_____

	Agree Strongly	Agree	Am Uncertain	Disagree	Disagree Strongly
13. Develop both basic and advanced skills in the chosen area of study	_____	_____	_____	_____	_____
14. Help students develop the attitudes and perspectives they need to do well in positions related to their chosen fields	_____	_____	_____	_____	_____
15. Teach the communication skills involved in getting along with superiors, subordinates, and colleagues	_____	_____	_____	_____	_____
16. Strengthen student vo-cational self-confidence	_____	_____	_____	_____	_____
17. Help students find them-selves	_____	_____	_____	_____	_____
18. Assist students in de-veloping leadership potential	_____	_____	_____	_____	_____

PART II.   BUSINESS ADMINISTRATION
          PROGRAM DETERMINANTS

19. The business adminis-tration faculty is qualified to help determine what courses to teach in busi-ness administration programs	_____	_____	_____	_____	_____
20. The business community is qualified to help de-termine what courses should be taught in busi-ness administration programs	_____	_____	_____	_____	_____

	Agree Strongly	Agree	Am Uncertain	Disagree	Disagree Strongly
21. The students enrolled in business administration programs are qualified to help determine what courses should be taught in business administration programs	_____	_____	_____	_____	_____

PART III. ADMISSION CRITERIA

	Agree Strongly	Agree	Am Uncertain	Disagree	Disagree Strongly
22. The admission of students into business administration programs should be based on previous school grade point averages, recommendations of faculty members, counselors, and school examinations, and/or other personal documentation	_____	_____	_____	_____	_____
23. The admission of students into business administration programs should largely be the responsibility of the business administration faculty	_____	_____	_____	_____	_____
24. The admission of students into business administration programs should be determined by the students themselves: they know best whether or not they are suited for such programs	_____	_____	_____	_____	_____

PART IV: INTERNSHIP/COOPERATIVE EXPERIENCES

	Agree Strongly	Agree	Am Uncertain	Disagree	Disagree Strongly
25. The business internship/ cooperative program within a business administration curriculum ought to be an integral part of a student's learning experience	_____	_____	_____	_____	_____

	Agree Strongly	Agree	Am Uncertain	Disagree	Disagree Strongly
26. The business internship/ cooperative positions that students secure while en- rolled in business adminis- tration programs are essen- tial in meeting the objec- tives of those programs	_____	_____	_____	_____	_____

PART V: THE FUNCTION OF THE BUSINESS
         ADMINISTRATION FACULTY

27. A primary function of the business administration fa- culty ought to be to pro- vide business administration students with vocational career counseling	_____	_____	_____	_____	_____
28. A primary function of the business administration faculty ought to be to counsel/advise students in selecting courses	_____	_____	_____	_____	_____
29. A primary function of the business administration faculty ought to be to work closely with the business community	_____	_____	_____	_____	_____

SECTION C

DIRECTIONS: Please answer each question by checking (✓) the space next to
             your choice. Unless you are specifically asked to do otherwise,
             choose the one answer reflecting your opinion most accurately.

30. Do you believe that business administration programs are preparing
    students for jobs for which they could not otherwise qualify?

    _____ (1) Yes

    _____ (2) No

    _____ (3) I don't know

31. In your opinion, are graduates of business administration programs better prepared for the business world than are those students graduating from nonbusiness degree programs?

_____ (1) Yes

_____ (2) No

_____ (3) I don't know

32. Are you currently employing, or have you previously employed, graduates of business administration programs?

_____ (1) Yes

_____ (2) No

_____ (3) I don't know

SECTION D

33. If you answered "NO" to any of the last three preceding questions, please explain your reasons below.

_____

_____

_____

_____

_____

_____

_____

_____

151

34. To what extent do you believe that business administration programs help students satisfy the requirements they must meet in order to be employed in responsible positions?

    _____ (1) Extremely helpful

    _____ (2) Helpful

    _____ (3) Minimally or not at all helpful

    _____ (4) I don't know

35. On the whole, how would you rate the quality of the business administration programs with which you have been involved professionally?

    _____ (1) Excellent

    _____ (2) Good

    _____ (3) Fair

    _____ (4) Poor

36. What changes would you make in college business administration programs in order to increase their value as learning experiences?

    _____

    _____

    _____

    _____

    _____

    _____

    _____

    _____

    _____

    _____

    _____

    _____

BIBLIOGRAPHY

Adames, Rafael S. "The Current Status and Future Directions of Distributive Education in New Hampshire." Ed.D dissertation, University of Massachusetts, May 1975.

AIR Summary Report: Survey and Assessment of the Status of Career Education in the Public Schools During 1974-1975. Palo Alto, Calif.: American Institutes for Research, 1976.

Argyris, Chris. Management and Organizational Development. New York: McGraw-Hill, 1971.

Bach, George L. "Whither Education for Business: 1950-2000?" AACSB Bulletin 11 (1975): 13.

Bailey, L. J., and R. W. Stadt. Career Education: New Approaches to Human Development. Bloomington, Ill.: McKnight, 1973.

Baker, Gus E. "The Teacher's Role in Career Education." School Shop 32 (1972): 35-37.

Banks, F. K., and M. C. Hillestad. Curricular Implications of Automated Data Processing for Educational Institutions. St. Peter, Minn.: Delta Pi Epsilon, 1968.

Basil, Douglas C. Managerial Skills for Executive Action. New York: American Management Association, 1970.

Becker, Selwyn W., and Duncan Neuhauser. The Efficient Organization. New York: Elsevier, 1975.

Beckett, John A. Management Dynamics: The New Synthesis. New York: McGraw-Hill, 1971.

Benson, A. H., and D. H. Blocher. "The Change Process Applied to Career Development Programs." Personnel and Guidance Journal 53 (1975): 656-62.

Benson, A. M. Implementing Career Education Programs. St. Paul: Minnesota Department of Education, 1975.

Berliner, Herman. "Real Economic Benefits of Higher Education." Personnel Journal, February 1971, p. 125.

Berry, D. "Management Education in American Schools." Economist, August 12, 1972, pp. 68-70.

Block, M. H. "Business Administration Transfer and Career Programs." National Business Education Quarterly 36 (December 1967): 52-57.

Bok, Derek. Quoted in "Graduates: Ill Prepared for Business?" Worcester Gazette (Massachusetts), March 30, 1979, p. 2.

Borland, David T. "Organizational Action Process." Address to the Annual Convention of the American College Personnel Association, Atlanta, Georgia, March 5-8, 1975, pp. 4-7.

Bowen, H. "Business Schools and the University—Opportunities for Reform." In Entrepreneurship and the Dynamics of the Educational Process, edited by C. C. Ling. St. Louis: American Association of Collegiate Schools of Business, 1969.

Brannen, T. R. "Stages and Problems of Curriculum Transition." AACSB Bulletin 5 (October 1968): 1-21.

Brown, Laurence A. Employment of an Open Learning Course with Traditional and Nontraditional Learners. Washington, D.C.: National Institute of Education, 1976.

Buckley, John W. "Programmed and Non-Programmed Instruction: Integration Criteria in Curriculum Design." Accounting Review, April 1959, p. 390.

Bulletin of Bryant College. Smithfield, R.I., 1980.

Burford, Roger L., and Donald R. Williams. "Quantitative Methods in the Undergraduate Curricula of AACSB Member Institutions." Decision Sciences 3 (January 1972): 111-27.

Business and Society Curriculum: A Position Paper. Prepared by the Governance Committee of the Social Issues in Management Division, The Academy of Management, January 1976.

Calhoun, Roger E. "The New Work Ethic." Training and Development Journal, May 1980, pp. 127-30.

Campbell, R. The Career Planning and Support System. Columbus, Ohio: Center for Vocational Education, 1975.

Career Education: What It Is and Why We Need It. Washington, D.C.: Chamber of Commerce of the United States, 1975.

Cayley, William E., and Thomas W. Harold. "Which Way in a Program Change, Content or Method? One Response." Collegiate News and Views 33 (Winter 1979-80): 13-18.

Cheit, Earl F. "What Is the Field of Business and Society and Where Is It Going?" Paper presented at a Business and Society Workshop: State of the Art and Program for the Future. Schools of Business Administration, March 23-26, 1975, Berkeley, California.

Chomitz, D. L. "Business Program Acceleration in the Junior College." Journal of Business Education 45 (1968): 337-39.

Clark, John J., and Blaise J. Opulente. The Impact of the Foundation Reports on Business Education. New York: St. John's University Press, 1963.

Clark, Robert B. "How Relevant Is Accounting Education?" The Journal of Accountancy, February 1973, pp. 90-91.

Clark, Robert P. "Business Enterprises Education Program: A Course for Supervisors." New Outlook, March 1974, pp. 128-31.

Cohen, Michael, and John N. Collins. "Some Correlates of Organization Effectiveness." Public Personnel Management 3 (November–December 1974): 493-99.

Conner, James E. "Business Broadens Its Support." College and University Journal 10 (May 1971): 8-9.

Cook, J., D. Stenning, and D. V. Tiedeman. Education for the Integration of Occupational Clusters into Careers. Information Series No. 3, CE 004 793. DeKalb, Ill.: ERIC Clearinghouse in Career Education, 1975.

Cooper, Robert. "Alienation from Work." New Society 30 (January 1969): 161-63.

Crawford, L. C. A Competency Pattern Approach to Curriculum Construction in Distributive Teacher Education. Washington, D.C.: U.S. Department of Health, Education and Welfare, 1967.

Cress, Carl C. "The Junior High School Business Curriculum." In The Business Curriculum, Sixth Yearbook, National Commercial Teachers Federation. Bowling Green, Ky.: The Federation, 1940.

Croteau, Maureen. "Deadends Waylay the Unwary Seeker." The Providence Sunday Journal (Rhode Island), November 25, 1979, p. E3.

Daughtrey, Anne C. Methods of Teaching Basic Business and Economic Education. Cincinnati, Ohio: South-Western, 1974.

Davis, Russell G., and Gary M. Lewis. Education and Employment. Lexington, Mass.: Lexington Books, 1975.

Deal, Emit B. "Business Core Curricula Revisited." Collegiate News and Views 30 (Spring 1977): 19-24.

Devlin, Thomas C. "Career Development Courses." Junior College Placement, Summer 1974, pp. 63-68.

Diaz, Luis C. "Human Resource Accounting: If You Please." Accountants Journal 24 (1974): 7-8.

Dieffenderfer, Richard, Lee Kopp, and Orest Cap. Business-Industry-Labor Linkages: A Handbook for Improving Personnel Development Programs. Columbus: Ohio State University, June 1977.

DiVincenti, Marie. Administering Nursing Service. Boston: Little, Brown, 1975.

Donovan, Marguerite E. "Business, Liberal Arts, and the Transfer Student." Journal of Business Education, January 1976, pp. 87-88.

Drucker, Peter F. Management. New York: Harper and Row, 1974.

Dubin, R., and J. E. Champous. "Central Life Interests and Job Satisfaction." Organizational Behavior and Human Performance 18 (1977): 366-77.

Dull, Lloyd W. "The Cluster Concept in Career Education." Educational Leadership 30 (1972): 218-21.

Dumphy, Philip W., ed. Career Development for the College Student. New York: Carroll Press, 1969.

Edge, Alfred G., and Ronald Greenwood. "How Managers Rank Knowledge, Skills, and Attributes Possessed by Business Administration Graduates." AACSB Bulletin 11 (October 1974): 30-34.

Edgeworth, H. C. "Curriculum Feedback." Collegiate News and Views, May 1971, pp. 13-15.

Educational Leadership 34 (October 1976), entire issue.

Elliott, Norman W. "Business Education: High Schools." Encyclopedia of Education, edited by Lee C. Eighton. New York: Macmillan and the Free Press, 1971.

Ellis, Mary L. A Report to the Nation on Vocational Education. Flagstaff: Northern Arizona University, November 1975.

Even, Brenda B. Integrating Career Education into Teacher Preparation. Washington, D.C.: U.S. Government Printing Office, 1976.

Fiber, Larry. "The Role of the Department Chairman at Different Levels of Business Education." Business Education Forum, May 1972, pp. 37-39.

Finch, C. R., and N. A. Sheppard. "Career Education Is Not Vocational Education." Journal of Career Education 2 (1975): 37-46.

Fischer, Frank E., and Lydia Strong. "Introduction: 'X Factor' in the Management Job." In Effective Communication on the Job, edited by Elizabeth Marting, Robert E. Finley, and Ann Ward, pp. 12-20. New York: American Management Association, 1963.

Flaumenhaft, Frank K. "The Undergraduate Curriculum in Business Education." Collegiate News and Views 31 (Fall 1977): 15-17.

Ford, Guy B. Building a Winning Employee Team. New York: American Management Association, 1964.

Fox, R. S. "Innovation Curriculum: An Overview." Interchange 3 (1972): 131-43.

"The Future of Management Education and the Role of the American Assembly of Collegiate Schools of Business: A Report of the AACSB Educational Innovation Committee," St. Louis, Mo., December 5, 1975.

Gentry, Lee, and Eileen Gentry. "Business Management Concept Areas for Two-Year Postsecondary Institutions." Business Education Forum, April 1978, pp. 37-38.

Gibbs, W. E., et al. "Comparative Study of Conventional Programmed Instruction in Bookkeeping." Journal of Educational Research 61 (1968): 320-23.

Gifford, John B., Robert L. Thornton, and H. Ralph Jones. "A Comparison of the Attitudes of Practitioners and Business Students toward Social and Economic Systems." Collegiate News and Views 32 (Fall 1978): 1-9.

Ginzberg, Eli. Career Guidance: Who Needs It, Who Provides It, Who Can Improve It. New York: McGraw-Hill, 1971.

Giusti, Joseph P., and George R. Lovette. "The Business School in Higher Education." Journal of Business Education, January 1971, p. 42.

Goddard, Merl L. The Potential Role of the Junior College in Education for Business. Cincinnati, Ohio: South-Western, 1967.

Goldhammer, Keith, and Robert E. Taylor, eds. Career Education: Perspective and Promise. Columbus, Ohio: Charles E. Merrill, 1972.

Gordon, Robert A., and James E. Howell. Higher Education for Business. New York: Columbia University Press, 1959.

Gould, Sammy, and William Litzinger. "A Perspective on Business Faculty Mobility." Collegiate News and Views 21 (Winter 1977-78): 11-14.

Graham, John E. "Competency-Based Accounting Instruction." Journal of Business Education, January 1977, pp. 184-86.

Graham, Robert, and Milton Valentine. "Alienation through Isolation." Personnel Administration 32 (March/April 1969): 16-20.

Gregoire, Roger. The University Teaching of Social Sciences: Business Management. Paris: United Nations Educational, Scientific, and Cultural Organization, 1966.

Gros, Ridley J. "The Communications Package in the Business Curriculum: Why?" ABCA Bulletin 39 (December 1976): 5-8.

Haas, K. B. Distributive Education: Organization and Administration. Vocational Education Bulletin No. 211. Washington, D.C.: U.S. Office of Education, 1940.

Hackman, J. Richard, and Greg R. Oldham. "Motivation through the Design of Work: Test of a Theory." Organizational Behavior and Human Performance 16 (August 1976): 250-79.

Hackman, J. Richard, and Mary Dean Lee. Redesigning Work: A Strategy for Change. Scarsdale, N.Y.: Work in America Institute, n.d.

Hagans, R. W. "What Is Experience-Based Career Education?" Illinois Career Education Journal 33 (Spring 1976): 6-10.

Hansen, Lorraine S. Career Education: Teachers' Responsibilities. Minneapolis: University of Minnesota, 1973.

_____. An Examination of the Definitions and Concepts of Career Education. Washington, D.C.: National Advisory Council for Career Education, June 1977.

Hanson, G. A., and E. C. Parker. "Simulated Work Experience for Prospective Business Teachers." National Business Education Quarterly 38 (December 1969): 25-34.

Harris, Norman C., and John F. Grede. Career Education in Colleges. San Francisco: Jossey-Bass, 1977.

Hart, Jerry C., and Sara A. Hart. "An Accounting Program Designed to Meet the Expectations of Accounting Educators and Practitioners." Collegiate News and Views 34 (Spring 1981): 19-22.

Hauser, Phillip M. "Education and Careers—Concordant or Disconcordant." Address to the National Meeting of the College Placement Council, May 28, 1975, Washington, D.C.

Havelock, R. G. A Guide to Innovation in Education. Ann Arbor: University of Michigan, 1970.

Haynes, B., and J. Graham. Research in Business Education. Los Angeles: C. C. Crawford, 1932.

Hensley, Gene, and Mark Schulman. Two Studies on the Role of Business and Industry and Participation in Career Education. Washington, D.C.: National Advisory Council for Career Education, June 1977, p. 5.

Herr, E. L. The Emerging History of Career Education: A Summary View. Washington, D.C.: National Advisory Council for Career Education, 1976.

_____. Review and Synthesis of Foundations for Career Education. Columbus: Center for Vocational and Technical Education, Ohio State University, 1972.

Hersey, Paul, and Kenneth H. Blanchard. Management of Organizational Behavior. Englewood Cliffs, N.J.: Prentice-Hall, 1969.

Hildebrandt, Herbert W., et al. "Proposal for a Master of Business Administration in Business Communication." ABCA Bulletin, March 1977, pp. 3-7.

Hilgert, Raymond L. "A Career Preparation Class for Business School Undergraduates." Collegiate News and Views 32 (Winter 1978-79): 1-4.

Hines, George. "Courses Recommended for Business Students by Managers and Educators: A Cross Cultural Study." Journal of Business, December 1971, pp. 12-20.

Holland, John L. Making Vocational Choices: A Theory of Careers. Englewood Cliffs, N.J.: Prentice-Hall, 1973.

Hoyt, Kenneth B. Career Education: Contributions to an Evolving Concept. Salt Lake City, Utah: Olympus, 1975.

_____. Career Education, Vocational Education and Occupational Education: An Approach to Defining Differences. Columbus, Ohio: Center for Vocational Education, May 1976.

_____. "Career Education and Work Experience Education: Can We Join Together?" Journal of Cooperative Education, November 1976, pp. 8-15.

_____. The Concept of Collaboration in Career Education. Washington, D.C.: U.S. Office of Education, Department of Health, Education and Welfare, 1979.

_____. Considerations of Career Education in Postsecondary Education. Washington, D.C.: HEW Monographs on Career Education, 1978.

_____. "An Introduction to Career Education: A Policy Paper of the U.S. Office of Education," HEW Publication no. (OE) 75-00504. Washington, D.C., n.d., pp. 8-13.

_____. The School Counselor and Career Education. Washington, D.C.: U.S. Government Printing Office, 1976.

Hoyt, Kenneth B., Ruppert H. Evans, Edward F. Mackin, and L. Garth. Career Education: What It Is and How to Do It. Salt Lake City, Utah: Olympus, 1972.

Huegli, Jon, and Harvey D. Tschirgi. "The Entry-Level Job—A Neglected Target for Our Business Schools." Collegiate News and Views 28 (Winter 1974-75): 21-23.

Isaacson, Lee E. Career Information in Counseling and Teaching. Boston: Allyn and Bacon, 1971.

James, Don L., and Ronald L. Decker. "Does Business Student Preparation Satisfy Personnel Officers?" Collegiate News and Views 27 (Spring 1974): 26-29.

Jesser, David L. Career Education: A Priority of the Chief State School Officers. Salt Lake City, Utah: Olympus, 1976.

Jones, Maloyd E., Jr. "Work Experience Programs in Business Education." Delta Pi Epsilon Journal, February 1973, pp. 22-32.

Kanter, R. M. "Work in a New America." Daedalus, Winter 1978, pp. 47-78.

Keefe, William F. Listen, Management: Creative Listening for Better Managing. New York: McGraw-Hill, 1971.

Kelly, R. L. "The Accounting Curriculum." National Business Education Quarterly 36 (December 1967): 25-32.

Kim, Paul. "Personal Economic Understanding and College Business and Economics Courses." Delta Pi Epsilon Journal 19 (April 1977): 22-35.

Kleinjans, E. K. "What Do You Mean—'Relevance'?" Education Digest 37 (1972): 36-38.

Knowles, Asa S., ed. Handbook of College and University Administration—Academic. New York: McGraw-Hill, 1970.

Knowles, Asa S., et al. Handbook of Cooperative Education. San Francisco: Jossey-Bass, 1971.

Koschler, T. A., and D. Owen. "Data Processing and Computer Programming Curriculum." National Business Education Quarterly 36 (December 1967): 38-41.

Krajewski, Lorraine A. "Business Educators as Futurists." Journal of Business Education, January 1977, pp. 173-74.

Krzystofik, Anthony T., and Spencer C. Bridgman. "A Need for Closer Integration of Two- and Four-Year Business Programs." Collegiate News and Views 34 (Spring 1981): 1-6.

Kuhlman, John M. "The Impact of Quantitative Analysis in the College of Business." Collegiate News and Views 15 (October 1961): 7-10.

LaDuca, A., and L. J. Barnett. "Career Education: Program on a White Horse." New York University Education Quarterly 5 (Spring 1974): 6-12.

Larson, Milton E. "Career Education's Most Vulnerable Front." American Vocational Journal 40 (1974): 43-44.

Lentilhon, Robert W. "Accounting Graduates Revisited." Collegiate News and Views 30 (Spring 1977): 13-14.

Lesikar, Raymond V. Business Communication: Theory and Application. Homewood, Ill.: Richard D. Irwin, 1972.

Lill, David J. "Using the Personnel Executive and the Delphi Technique to Develop a Model Marketing Curriculum." Address given to the Southern Marketing Association Meeting, November 15, 1974, Atlanta, Georgia.

Locker, Kitty. "Making Business Communication Courses Academically Respectable." ABCA Bulletin, March 1979, pp. 6-10.

Lomax, P. S., and W. H. Wilson. Improving Research in Business Education. Monograph 105. Cincinnati, Ohio: South-Western, 1962.

Lumsden, George J. Impact Management. New York: AMACOM, A Division of American Management Association, 1979.

Lyons, Edward H., and James H. Wilson. Work-Study College Programs. New York: Harper and Brothers, 1961.

Maanen, John Van, Edgar H. Schrein, and Lottie Bailyn. "The Shape of Things to Come: A New Look at Organizational Careers." In Managing Career Development, edited by Marilyn A. Morgan, pp. 3-12. New York: D. Van Nostrand, 1980.

Mali, Paul. Managing by Objectives. New York: Wiley-Interscience, 1972.

Maslow, A. H. "A Theory of Human Motivation." Psychological Review 50 (1943): 370-96.

Mason, R. E., and P. G. Haines. Cooperative Occupational Education. Danville, Ill.: Interstate Printers and Publishers, 1972.

Mathis, Edward J. "A Survey of Economics Curricula in AACSB Accredited Schools of Business Administration." Collegiate News and Views 34 (Spring 1981): 15-17.

McClure, Larry, and Carolyn Buan, eds. Essays on Career Education. Portland Oreg.: Northwest Regional Education Laboratory, 1973.

McGuire, Joseph W. "The Collegiate Business School Today: Whatever Happened to the World We Knew?" Collegiate News and Views 25 (Spring 1972): 1-5.

McKinney, L. A., et al. Career Education Personnel Development. Columbus, Ohio: Center for Vocational Education, July 1975.

McKitrick, Max O. "Consumer Relations: A New Curriculum for Collegiate Schools of Business." Journal of Business Education, May 1977, pp. 350-52.

_____. "A Survey of Corporate Consumer Relations Managers and Their Evaluations of a Collegiate Consumer Relations Curriculum." Kalamazoo: Department of Business Education and Administrative Services, Western Michigan University, 1976.

McLaughlin, D. H. Career Education in the Public Schools, 1974-1975: A National Survey. Washington, D.C.: U.S. Government Printing Office, 1976.

Meyer, Marshal W. Environments and Organizations. San Francisco: Jossey-Bass, 1978.

Miles, Benton E. "Developing Distributive Education Programs." In Curriculum Development in Education for Business, edited by James W. Crews and Z. S. Dickerson, Jr., pp. 175-87. Reston, Va.: National Business Education Association, 1977.

Miller, Donald S. "Alternative Approaches to Effective Business Programs." Collegiate News and Views 32 (Winter 1978-79): 9-12.

Nash, Robert J., and Russell M. Agne. "A Case of Misplaced Relevance." Journal of Teacher Education 24 (1973): 87-89.

National Advisory Council for Career Education. Interim Report with Recommendations for Legislation. Washington, D.C.: U.S. Government Printing Office, 1975.

National Commission for Cooperative Education. Undergraduate Programs of Cooperative Education. Boston: Northeastern University, 1977.

Nistal, Gerard E. "Is Higher Education Responsive to the Needs of the Real World of Business?" Collegiate News and Views 33 (Winter 1979-80): 7-11.

Nollen, Stanley. New Patterns of Work. Scarsdale, N.Y.: Work in America Institute, n.d.

Nord, Daryl, and Tom Seymour. "Yes! The Business Department Teaches Data Processing." Balance Sheet, March 1978, pp. 282-84.

Oliver, A. I. Curriculum Improvement. New York: Dodd, Mead, 1965.

Pierson, Frank C., et al. A Study of University-College Programs in Business Administration. New York: McGraw-Hill, 1959.

Pierson, Frank C., et al. The Education of American Businessmen: A Study of University College Programs in Business Administration. New York: McGraw-Hill, 1959.

Podell, Joel, Abraham Axelrod, Jonas Falik, and Dennis Green. "The Introductory College Business Course: A New Dimension." Journal of Business Education, May 1977, pp. 352-54.

Popham, Estelle L. "Making Business Education Meaningful with a Competency-Based Curriculum." Business Education World, vol. 55, no. 5 (May-June 1975).

Popham, J. W. An Evaluation Guide Book. Los Angeles: Instructional Objectives Exchange, 1971.

Pratt, Christopher G. L. Cooperative Education. Trenton, N.J.: Trenton State College, 1973.

_____. "Survey of Attitudes toward Cooperative Education." Journal of Cooperative Education 16 (1979): 32-37.

_____. "Survey of Faculty Attitudes toward Cooperative Education." Journal of Cooperative Education 16 (May 1974): 68-79.

Prewitt, Lean B. "Research in Office Practice." Office Practice Program in Business Education (Somerville, Mass., Eastern Business Teachers Association) 46 (1969): 33.

Rainey, B. G. "Articulation in Collegiate Education for Business." Ph.D. dissertation, University of Oklahoma, 1964.

Rall, Clifford L., and Frank E. O'Brien. Methods and Procedures for Job Identification and Placement Based upon Industrial Needs. Washington, D.C.: Office of Education, August 21, 1977.

Rand, James F. "Accountability Management and Productivity Bargaining." Personnel Journal, March 1978, pp. 154-58.

Rapp, M. A., and J. E. Barber. Career Education: Plans and Programs of the States, 1976. Moravia, N.Y.: Chronicle Guidance Publications, 1976.

Renwick, Patricia A., and Edward E. Lawler. "What You Really Want from Your Job." Psychology Today 11 (May 1978): 53-118.

Reschke. Claus. "Career Education at the College Level: A Modest Proposal." Paper presented at the Annual Meeting of the American Association of Teachers of German, August 1976, Philadelphia.

Reynolds, R. John, and E. Michael Walsh. "The Bachelor's Degree in Technical Careers: Business Options for the Vocational-Technical Associate Degree Graduate." Collegiate News and Views 31 (Winter 1977-78): 15-17.

Rosow, Jerome M. "Quality of Work Life Issues for the 1980s." Training and Development Journal, March 1981, pp. 33-52.

Rossi, Peter H., Howard E. Freeman, and Sonia R. Wright. Evaluation: A Systematic Approach. London: Sage Publications, 1979.

Schein, Edgar H. "Changing Role of the Personnel Manager." Keynote address at the CUPA Eastern Regional Convention, April 1975, Newton, Mass.

Schmidt, Richard J. "The Two-Year Accounting Graduate—Education and Job Functions." Collegiate News and Views 33 (Winter 1979-80): 1-6.

Sexton, Robert F., and Richard A. Ungerer. Rationales for Experiential Education. ERIC Higher Education Research Report No. 3. Washington, D.C.: American Association for Higher Education, 1975.

Sinetar, Marsha. "Management in the New Age: An Exploration of Changing Work Values." Personnel Journal, September 1980, pp. 749-55.

Steiner, George. "Future Curricula in Schools of Management." AACSB Bulletin 13 (October 1976): 7-12.

Stevenson, Gloria. "Evaluating Training Daily." Training and Development Journal, May 1980, pp. 120-22.

Stevick, Arlo D. Model for Small Business Management Program in North Dakota Post-Secondary Institutions. Bismarck: North Dakota State Board for Vocational Education, July 1978.

Stroh, Thomas F. Managing the New Generation in Business. New York: McGraw-Hill, 1971.

"Suggestions for the New Business Communication Teacher." ABCA Bulletin, September 1975, p. 32.

Super, D. E. Career Education and the Meaning of Work. Washington, D.C.: U.S. Government Printing Office, 1976.

Sutherland, Alphonzo. "An Evaluation of Individualized Instruction for Evening/Part-Time Students of Business." Practicum presented to Nova University in partial fulfillment of the requirements for the Doctor of Education degree, Fort Lauderdale, Fla., May 1975.

Sweetland, John. Occupational Stress and Productivity. Scarsdale, N.Y.: Work in America Institute, n.d.

Thomas, Joe. "Operating Characteristics of Cooperative Education Programs in Business Schools." Journal of Cooperative Education 16 (1979): 31-35.

Tiedeman, D. V. "Structuring Personal Integration into Career Education." Personnel and Guidance Journal 53 (May 1975): 706-11.

Tjornhom, S. A. "Business Curriculum Pattern in Selected Public Junior Colleges in the United States." Ph.D. dissertation, University of North Dakota, 1967.

Trimpe, A. "Distributive Education at the Postsecondary Level." Business Education Forum 23 (January 1969): 26-28.

Tyler, Ralph W. Basic Principles of Curriculum and Instruction. Chicago: University of Chicago Press, 1949.

Valley, John R. "Experiential Education and the Nontraditional Student." In Dimensions of Experiential Education, edited by Robert F. Sexton. Washington, D.C.: National Center for Public Service Internships, 1976.

Van Pelt, James C., and Edwin C. Spencer. "The Quantitative Curricula of AACSB Accredited Undergraduate Business Schools." AACSB Bulletin, Spring 1977, pp. 11-16.

Wakin, B. Bertha. "Competency-Based Teacher Education: Boon or Bane in Business Education Programs ?" Journal of Business Education 53 (January 1978): 170-71.

Wallace, Andrew C. "Education in Business Administration: Image and Implication." Collegiate News and Views 25 (Spring 1972): 4.

Warr, P., ed. Personal Goals and Work Design. London: Wiley, 1976.

Watson, Frank. An Analysis of the Business Curriculum. Cincinnati, Ohio: South-Western, 1966.

Wharton, Clifton R. "Career Education at the College Level." Today's Education, April-May 1976, pp. 74-77.

"What's New in Career Development." Career Development Bulletin 1 (Spring 1979): 1.

White, M. A., and J. Duker. "Models of Schooling and Models of Evaluation." Teachers College Record 74 (1973): 293-307.

Winn, Paul R., and Ross H. Johnson. "Sequencing Quantitative Topics in a Business Curriculum." AACSB Bulletin 9 (January 1973): 10-14.

Work in America. Report for the Department of Health, Education and Welfare. Cambridge, Mass.: MIT Press, 1976.

Worker Alienation. Scarsdale, N.Y.: Work in America Institute, n.d.

Yankelovich, Daniel. "The New Psychological Contracts at Work." Psychology Today 2 (May 1978): 46-50.

INDEX

ABOUT THE AUTHOR

DONALD L. JOYAL is Professor of Human Resource Management and Organizational Behavior and serves as Associate Chairman for the Department of Management at Worcester State College located at Worcester, Massachusetts. He serves as a lecturer of management at Bryant College at Smithfield, Rhode Island, and is on the adjunct faculty for the COPACE program at Clark University in Worcester, Massachusetts.

Dr. Joyal has authored a number of articles on management, communication, and motivation. These articles reflect his extensive experience as a management and educational consultant in the private and public sector.

Dr. Joyal holds a number of degrees from various educational institutions throughout the country. He has a Bachelor of Science in management from New Hampshire College; a Master of Business Administration in management from Bryant College; a Master of Arts in Education from Suffolk University; a Certificate of Advanced Graduate Study in Educational Administration from the State College at Boston; and a Doctor of Business Administration in Organizational Behavior and Management from Western Colorado University.

Dr. Joyal was selected as an Outstanding Young Man of America for 1981. This nomination recognizes young men throughout the nation for their professional achievement and community service. He was awarded the General Electric Corporation Fellowship in Career Development offered by Boston University School of Education and is also listed in Who's Who in Training and Development.